Columbia

Columbia

GREAT RIVER OF THE WEST

Earl Roberge

CHRONICLE BOOKS

Printed in Japan by Dai Nippon Printing Co. Ltd., Tokyo.

Library of Congress Cataloging in Publication Data

Roberge, Earl, 1918–
    Columbia, great river of the West.

    Includes index.
    1. Columbia River — History. 2. Columbia River —
Description and travel. 1. Title.
F853.R63 1985   979.7   85-11022
ISBN 0-87701-336-5

Book and cover design: Paula Schlosser
Composition: TBH/Typecast, Inc.

CHRONICLE BOOKS
One Hallidie Plaza
San Francisco, CA 94102

Contents

To Donald Paul Hodel, administrator, outdoorsman, whitewater kayaker and wonderful companion, this work is respectfully dedicated.

At Castlegar, British Columbia, the Columbia changes from a strictly scenic to a working river. This pulp mill is the first of a series stretching almost all the way to the mouth of the River.

Foreword

FOR MORE THAN THIRTY-FOUR YEARS, ever since he first saw the Columbia Gorge sheathed in the shimmering splendor of a silver thaw, Earl Roberge has carried on a shameless love affair with the Columbia River. Here, at last, is a paean to that love, brilliantly portrayed in the stunning color photographs that are his trademark, and prose which, inspired by the beauty of his subject, often becomes lyrical.

From its source in an icy Canadian lake to its mouth in the broad Pacific, he has traveled its length many times by boat, car, and foot, thereby acquiring a first-hand knowledge of the Great River of the West that results in this, the definitive book on a majestic region.

The Columbia is more than just a great river, it is the vital, pulsing artery of the Pacific Northwest and the silent witness to its history and development. In painstaking detail, bolstered by research that has taken him as far afield as London, England, for a look at the archives of the great British trading companies that first opened up the country, the author has traced the geological, political, and economic growth of a vitally diverse region, and the part the great river has had in its development. The beauty of the wild upper reaches of the Columbia, a region unchanged from the time of Columbus, the stark grandeur of the desert country, and the energy developed by this, the world's most energy-productive stream, are all portrayed in words and photographs that achieve true artistic merit.

Whether your interest is in the River's picturesque past or equally dramatic present, this book is for you. You are present at the River's long delayed discovery and are part of the struggle between England and the United States for the possession of the Oregon Country. You hear the lilting boat songs of the voyageurs shooting the rapids in their fur-laden bateaux, and endure the trials of the pioneers who braved the Oregon Trail. You watch the transformation of a desolate, arid region into a garden through the miracle of irrigation and electrical generation. You take part in the railroad wars and the robust days of steamboating. Like the thousands of workers who built the Hanford Engineering Works, you wonder just what it is you are building in the desert and ponder the consequences for good or evil of the Atomic Age that was engendered here. You face the problems, past, present, and future, that are so much a part of the energy developed along the River. And when you are through, you will understand why the River casts such a potent spell and will yourself gladly surrender to its enchantment.

Introduction

SOMEWHERE ON AN UNNAMED SLOPE, a snowflake melts and forms a single drop of water. Joined by myriad of its kind and following an inexorable law of Nature, it trickles down the precipitous slope of its Canadian mountain birthplace, is absorbed into a rocky fissure, and finally emerges as a crystal clear, icy cold spring flowing into an aquamarine lake.

And so the Columbia River is born.

Before the waters born here reach the Pacific Ocean, over twelve hundred miles away at Astoria, they will have washed the feet of snow-clad peaks, mirrored forests little changed since the time of Columbus, and crashed through rapids littered with the bones of those who had the temerity to challenge their might. They will have flowed through pellucid lakes of transcendental beauty, reflected gaunt basalt cliffs terrifying in their starkness, and have lost the chill of their glacial birth to the awesome intensity of a pitiless desert sun. They will have helped light cities, transform worthless desert into verdant gardens, refine metals, and carried on their broad back the burden of the empire they helped create. They will have

Sunset on the Columbia River with Mt. Hood in the background.

spun a dozen sets of turbines, helped cool the elemental heat of the atom, and shaped the destinies not only of cities, but also of the men and women living along the River's banks. They will have supported a life cycle reaching back thousands of years and have been a silent witness to history, for in few places in the world has a river more strongly influenced the course of events or been a more pervasive force in shaping its own destiny.

And when, at last, it breaks through its final mountain barrier and merges with the sea, it is only a matter of time before the cosmic forces of nature assert themselves and the process is repeated again, and again, and again, dwarfing in the majesty of their eternal rhythm the puny efforts of man . . . who has, nevertheless, achieved some degree of mastery over the mighty River and bent it to his will.

Any one of the great rivers of the world has its own personality, something that makes it unique, set apart from any other. But no river on Earth with the possible exception of the Nile or the Hohang-ho has it in the same degree as the stream that flows from Columbia Lake.

This, then, is the river of our story.

It would be patently futile to try to tell, in one book — or one lifetime — the whole story of a force as elemental as a mighty river, for this would be the chronicle of a living entity that has existed for eons, shaped the lives of uncounted generations of men and women, and profoundly affected the course of history. Rather, I would prefer to tell you what I saw, felt, and experienced in my many journeys up and down this noble river. And I will do so willingly, for I freely admit that since that first view, in January 1946, of the Columbia Gorge sheathed in the shimmering glow of a silver thaw, I have been hopelessly under the spell that the River weaves so effortlessly. It is a spell compounded of beauty and majesty: a rather potent combination, and one to which I am particularly susceptible. So this will be primarily an eyewitness report; and when I must rely on other witnesses who came before my time, I have trust in the potency of that same spell, secure in the knowledge that the enchantment of the Columbia is ageless, and I am not the first — or the last — to succumb to it.

The Columbia rises at Canal Flats in British Columbia at an elevation of 2,650 feet above sea level and flows 1,264 miles to the Pacific Ocean at Astoria, Oregon. It is the largest stream in the Pacific Northwest and the second largest in the United States in volume of water, being exceeded only by the Mississippi. Since it is at birth a Canadian river, it is only fair to report that it is exceeded in size by two other Canadian rivers: the majestic St. Lawrence, flowing into the Atlantic Ocean, and the Mackenzie, emptying its huge flood of ice cold water into the Artic Ocean. The Columbia drains an area of 259,000 square miles and is the greatest generator of electrical energy in North America, and possibly the world.

Somehow, mere statistics seem as pitifully inadequate in describing the grandeur of a river as they are in describing, say, a truly gorgeous woman. One may form a mental picture from the figures given, and even be reasonably close, but nothing takes the place of actually seeing those statistics transformed into a concrete fact that can be seen with actual eyes rather than with those of the mind. A good photograph comes close, and for that reason I painstakingly carried and used several cameras the length of the River, from its source to the mouth, not only once, but several times, for the Columbia is too multifaceted to be fully understood or appreciated on brief contact. It is several rivers, and each one can change its mood several times in one day, or even an hour. Each has its own personality, its own feeling, and its own fascination, but they all have one trait in common: each one, invariably, possesses a rare and unique beauty.

Beauty, of course, is an attribute common to many rivers, but the Columbia has it in such diversity that it stands pretty much in a class by itself. It is, in turn, a placid meandering stream flowing through a gentle countryside, a brawling, muscular mountain stream exuberantly charging through steep canyons, a tranquil series of quiet lakes mirroring glaciated mountains, and a deep-flowing, sullen stream broiling under a desert sun. In color, it may be a milky green, laden with glacial silt, a deep blue, or a dark blue-grey. In some stretches it is crystal clear, in others murky with a heavy load of suspended topsoil. In its lower stretches it flows with deceptively silent intensity, but no one knowledgeable about it even forgets for one minute its awesome power, for it is one of the greatest forces on the face of this earth, and its strength, though partially controlled by man, has never been completely overcome.

Because of the River's profound effect on

the region, it can very aptly be said that the Columbia is the string on which the events of Northwest history are strung like beads. The search for the legendary River of the West which geographers insisted must be in this section of the continent was one of the main reasons for early exploration. Once it was discovered, it became the highway that made exploration of these new domains possible, and its banks became the stage on which the international drama resulting therefrom was played out. The Columbia is far more than simply the largest stream in the Northwest: it is also its main artery, pulsating with the life blood of the whole region.

Just as the Northwest is the newest portion of the contiguous United States, the last explored and last settled, the Columbia is geologically a young river. While a river is admittedly a living entity, constantly changing its bed, banks, and channels, it usually settles down and becomes a sedate old lady, flowing through a stabilized landscape, even though it may occasionally kick up its heels. The Hudson, for instance, or the Connecticut, despite occasional lapses, are geologically middle aged.

Not so the Columbia. Its bed has been shaped by the usual forces of nature: fire, flood, wind, and rain, and especially ice; but some of these changes are so recent that the River can only be classified as in its geological youth. The last great natural cataclysm that shaped the River, the great ice dams attendant to the end of the last Ice Age, happened only some fifteen thousand years ago. Man, too, has done his best to change the Columbia to suit his needs, and while his comparatively puny efforts have been antlike compared to the massive earth movements occasioned by the southward march of the glaciers, still he has changed the littoral, and some of the changes he has achieved have materially altered the character of the river.

In the Grand Coulee and throughout the adjacent country clear to the base of the Cascades, the march of the glaciers has left its mark. The River once flowed through the Grand Coulee: a fantastic cataract, fed by the partially melting though advancing glaciers, whose volume was at least forty times that of the present stream. Near Brewster, Washington, the banks of the Columbia for some considerable distance are littered with *nomads*: huge boulders, some weighing thousands of tons, that were the cutting tools embedded in ploughshares of ice that

remorselessly gouged out the lake beds of Chelan, Kootenay, and Slocan, some of them hundreds of feet below sea level. Along canyon walls, long parallel grooves testify to the fantastic forces at work when the glaciers' ponderous bulk ground relentlessly onward, shaping the land and bequeathing to it a character that would profoundly influence the lives of countless generations yet unborn.

If we were to pick out one characteristic of the Columbia that makes it distinctive among the rivers of the world, it would have to be its power. It has several other attributes: its coldness, its clarity, its beauty; but in power it stands head and shoulders above any other river on Earth, and this feature more than any other has affected its destiny.

Considering that the Columbia in its first 120 miles falls only four inches per mile and the last 150 miles is a tidal river with very little fall, it is easily seen that the main drop, almost 2,500 feet, occurs in roughly 900 miles. Add to this the impressive statistic that the Columbia carries the second largest volume of water of any stream in the United States, and it easily becomes apparent why the Columbia is capable of generating more electrical power than any other stream in this country.

The Columbia River drainage is larger than France and England combined. Containing as it does several mountain ranges heavy with glaciers, it is also unique in that its heaviest flow comes during the summer months, a most fortuitous circumstance that has made irrigation in the Columbia Basin feasible. By the time the river reaches its mouth, there are, mingled in its depths, waters that originated as far south as Nevada, as far east as Wyoming, and as far north as the borders of Alberta. It will have flowed through regions dominated by ice, through scorching deserts where the River's volume is measurably reduced by evaporation, and finally through a region of rain forest tropical in its luxuriance.

Originating as it does in the glaciers of British Columbia and the Rocky Mountains, it is no wonder that the Columbia is by far the coldest of our major rivers. It is also the least polluted, for only in its lower stretches does it flow through any area of significant population. These are important factors, for many industries require pure water as much as they do electrical energy. In this latter requirement, the Columbia stands second to none.

It has been estimated that the total power potential of the world generated by the weight and flow of water is somewhere around 750,000,000 horsepower. Of this, one fifth, or 150,000,000 horsepower, is in North America. The Columbia alone contains 50,000,000 horsepower, or one third of the whole potential of the American sector of the Northern Hemisphere. It is probably the most productive stream in the world in terms of electrical energy, although the Soviet Union's gigantic plants on the Yenisey River may someday cause that stream to catch up with it.

The fact that the Columbia is so well adapted to the production of electrical energy has been the significant factor in its development. Not so long ago, the Columbia was a wild, scenic river draining an undeveloped wilderness. It has become, in the span of a few lifetimes, a major artery of commerce, a source of energy fostering one of the world's highest technological developments, and the progenitor of an agricultural miracle whose import is barely yet appreciated, even by those living right next to it.

The Spaniards, whose caravels and galleons ranged the oceans of the world during the golden days of their empire, probably were the first to confirm that the great River of the West was more than a myth. At the end of the eighteenth century, the balance of world power was slipping away from Spain, whose empire had reached its zenith, and was tipping toward the ascendant Great Britain. However, a most fortuitous circumstance helped those who so zealously sought to add luster to the Spanish crown. France and England were embroiled in a war with the rebellious English colonies on the east coast of North America, and Spain was accordingly left with a clear field. The same incandescent spirit that had burned so brightly in the breast of the conquistadores still animated the sons of Castile, and so the keels of their ships plowed many a strange ocean, ranged upward from Mexico, and affixed to the capes and headlands along the California and Oregon coast Spanish names that exist to this day. In 1774 the Spanish explorer Juan Perez discovered Queen

PREVIOUS PAGE. *Winter on the Upper Columbia, near Golden, British Columbia.*

Charlotte Island, sailing unknowingly past the mouth of the Columbia, and showed the path for the next, more successful explorer.

In 1775 Bruno Heceta, in a well-equipped expedition, sailed as far north as the Straits of Juan de Fuca. Losing part of his crew to hostile Indians at Destruction Island off the Olympic Peninsula, he sailed southward and on August 15, 1775 reached latitude 46° 10'N. There he made a very interesting discovery. The water was different in color than the usual ocean water, and the large bay in front of his ship was edged with breakers of prodigious size.

Heceta was a good sailor and a very skilled navigator. The observations he made of capes and headlands, done with the comparatively crude instruments of his day, are remarkably accurate, so we can safely assume that he actually saw the famed Columbia Bar, the entrance to the Columbia River, the middle of which lies at 46° 7'N. He also accurately described the two capes that border the bar, naming them Cabo de Frondoso (Leafy Cape), now Point Adams, and Cabo de San Roque, now Cape Hancock. Thinking the entrance itself to be a bay, he named it Ensenada de Ascuncion (Ascension Bay). For years, Spanish charts designated the river as Rio de San Roque.

For two days, Heceta sought to break through the murderous bar and finally gave up, partly because his depleted crew could not efficiently perform the extremely difficult navigation needed to get into such a powerful river.

The lengthy entries in his ship's log and the meticulously detailed descriptions he gives prove beyond a doubt that Bruno Heceta came within a mile or two of becoming the discoverer of the Columbia River. Had his crew not been decimated by Indians, he might have succeeded in crossing the bar, and the course of history could have been altered. As it was, Heceta's voyage formed the main claim that Spain held to the Oregon Country, a claim ceded to the United States in the treaty of 1819.

Capt. James Cook, Britain's equivalent of Christopher Columbus, sought in vain for the fabled River of the West. In his journeys up and down the Oregon Coast he must have passed and repassed the River's mouth, yet he failed to find either it or the Strait of Juan de Fuca. He did something, though, that was to have a tremendous impact on the history of the Northwest.

One of his stops was at Nootka Bay, on Vancouver Island. There, for a few iron nails, his crew acquired from the natives pelts of the sea otter. The thick, richly lustrous furs were used by his crew as bedding and were in pretty sad shape by the time they arrived in Canton, China. Nevertheless, they were, almost accidentally, sold there at a trememdous profit. Overnight, an overwhelming demand for peltries was created.

The Russians had already begun a fur trade with China, largely from their outposts on the Kamchatka Peninsula, but it was a desultory operation that never quite caught on. Not so the present fur craze. Ships began to converge on the Oregon Coast, trading cheap trinkets to the natives for furs worth a king's ransom. With the end of the American Revolution, Yankee skippers, who could smell a profit on the Oregon Coast clear from Boston, entered the trade with so much energy that in a comparatively short time they edged out the British, French, Spanish, and Russian competition and became the dominant faction on the Pacific Coast.

But still, in spite of all the traffic up and down the coast, the Columbia River remained undiscovered, a will-o'-the-wisp as elusive as the fabled Seven Cities of Cíbola.

On June 29, 1788, Capt. John Meares, an Englishman sailing under the Portuguese flag, attempted to find the river described by Heceta. At latitude 46° 10′N, he found "a deep bay . . . and a furious line of breakers." With a timidity not usually associated with British explorers, Meares gave up his quest and entered in his ship's log the notation: "We can now assert that there is no such river as the St. Roc, as laid down in Spanish charts." It is interesting to note that in spite of the negative opinion he evinced, Meares' "discovery" was one of the major arguments Great Britain advanced to bolster her claim to the Oregon Country.

Spain and Great Britain, which each claimed Nootka by right of discovery, had finally amicably settled their disputes by the treaty of 1791. The British sent there, as their commissioner, the legendary Capt. George Vancouver, who was not only a born explorer but also a man familiar with these waters. With all the attention the Oregon Country had been getting lately and with many puzzles about it still unsolved, Vancouver had instructions from his superiors not only to meticulously map the coast of Oregon and the Straits of Juan de Fuca but also, and above all, to find the mercurial River of the West. Vancouver was eminently well suited for his job, and his ship, the war sloop *Discovery*, was probably the best equipped vessel ever to sail these waters up to that time. If anyone could do it, Vancouver was that man, or so it seemed.

Enter into our story—and history—Capt. Robert Gray of Boston. Although still in his thirties, this canny New England skipper was already a veteran fur trader, having first seen the coast of Oregon in 1788. There, he traded a simple iron chisel for furs worth $8,000. The import of this transaction was not lost on him, especially when he realized that those already scandalous profits could be pyramided by further trade with the Orient. He spent eight months fur trading on the coast, then another six months in the long voyage to Canton, where he took on a cargo of silk, tea, spices, and other Oriental exotica. Still sailing westward, he headed for Boston and a place in history, for his ship, the *Lady Washington*, was the first American vessel to circumnavigate the globe. But history was not yet done with Robert Gray.

On April 27, 1792, Vancouver passed a cape in latitude 46° 19′N and surmised this must be the "Cape Disappointment" mentioned by Meares. He was aware, of course, that Heceta had claimed there was a large river in these latitudes, but he also knew that Meares had investigated this area and concluded that there was "no river here." In his mind, that settled it. It was preposterous to think that a British sailor could be wrong, and a Spaniard right. He sailed on.

That bit of chauvinism cost him an even higher place in history than he presently occupies and had a definite effect on the future history of the Pacific Northwest, for a few days later, Capt. Robert Gray, captain of the ship *Columbia Rediviva*, came by this same place. He remembered Heceta's findings and attached some importance to them, for he obviously had more respect for the Spaniard's observations than Vancouver had. On reaching 45° 10′N, he found a line of breakers as described by Heceta, and for nine days sought to breach them—unsuccessfully. The River was in full flood and the breakers at such times often reach a height of twenty feet.

Sailing in a northerly direction, he caught up with the *Discovery*. In reviewing his log with

Vancouver, he mentioned he had attempted to breach the mouth of Heceta's river and was patronizingly assured by the British captain that the river existed only as a figment of Spanish imagination.

Gray returned to the mouth of the Columbia, while Vancouver continued his explorations of the Straits of Juan de Fuca where, to his great chagrin, he found the Spaniards had preceded him.

On May 11, 1792, the day dawned clear with light winds and a favorable sea, revealing a channel obviously deep enough for Gray's ship. The time, the tide, the weather, everything was right. With characteristic daring, the young captain ordered all sails set and, hugging the shore, boldly sailed in. By ten o'clock he found himself in a large river of fresh water, a good fifteen miles from the sea.

The riddle of the Pacific Coast had been solved. The Columbia River had been found.

Gray named the river Columbia after his ship and moved fifteen more miles upstream, doing a brisk fur business with curious and friendly natives until May 20, when he cleared the bar and sailed northward. At Nootka Bay he prudently left an account of his discovery and a sketch of the River's mouth with Quadra, the Spanish commander.

There is some question as to whether Vancouver found out about the River's discovery from Gray himself or from Quadra, but there is no doubt that he was deeply chagrined to find that the brash young American had achieved a triumph that he himself so avidly sought. Nevertheless, he decided to salvage as much glory as the circumstances would permit by ordering his second in command, Lieutenant Broughton, to take the *Chatham* as far up the River as possible. This Broughton did, sailing his ship about twenty miles up river, then proceeding by cutter to a spot near the present site of Washougal.

The bitter disappointment of the British officers is evident in Broughton's report, for in every way he sought to demean Gray's discovery. The true mouth of the River, he reports, is some miles above the spot reached by Gray; this completely overlooks the fact that Gray had filled his casks with fresh water from the River. The width of the River is given by Broughton as a quarter of a mile, whereas in truth there is scarcely any spot on the mainstream of the Columbia below Longview that is less than a half mile wide; and in the lower stretches where

Broughton was cruising, it is in many places as much as two miles in width. Also, Broughton made a point of anchoring the *Chatham* twenty miles upriver, largely to prove that the Columbia was not navigable by oceangoing vessels. Gray, he claimed, had discovered a bay, not a river.

In view of the fact that Broughton's trip up the Columbia became a strong point in Britain's claim to the territory, these observations are of considerable interest. He took no chances, bestowing on the snow-clad peak towering over the River the name of a British admiral who had been second in command of a fleet against the rebellious English colonies on the East Coast, and nailing up proclamations claiming all this land for His Britannic Majesty "because he had no reason to believe that the subjects of any other civilized nation or state had ever entered this river before." From the very beginning, the contention of the United States and Great Britain for this land was marked by a decided coolness.

Gray apparently didn't attach as much importance to his discovery as did others, but it was to have far-reaching consequences. Without it, the claims of the fledgling United States to the West Coast would have been seriously jeopardized, for without the solid moral foundation provided by the right of discovery, it is doubtful that the American public would have so enthusiastically pressed its claim. Lack of moral grounds do not always sway the decisions of the mighty but their presence certainly helps to bolster a position, especially when that position is a highly popular one.

One person who did appreciate the full import of Gray's discovery was Thomas Jefferson, statesman, intellectual, dreamer . . . and President of the United States. Even before he consummated the Louisiana Purchase in 1803, Jefferson had been planning an expedition to find out if it were possible to reach the western shores of the continent by land, for this farsighted statesman had long held a dream far beyond the concept of most Americans, many of whom thought the natural western border of the United States should be the Mississippi River.

Jefferson, in his dream, saw a nation stretching from coast to coast, a vast nation epitomizing the ideals so dearly bought in the battles of the Revolution and fated to become one of the greatest powers on Earth. The Louisiana Purchase gave him legal right to the Mississippi drainage, and that, according to current knowledge gleaned from the hardy few who had been there, meant to the peaks of the Great Divide. Beyond that was unknown land at whose far edge an intrepid Bostoner had firmly planted the Stars and Stripes.

FEW EXAMPLES OF human endeavor have ever captured the imagination more thoroughly than the Lewis and Clark expedition, or been better chronicled. Here was a journey into the unknown by a small party of exuberant young men, officially eager to find out what their country had bought for $15 million, but unofficially off on a great adventure. The chance to see new scenes, to every day tread ground that had never before known the foot of a white man, appealed strongly to the pioneer spirit so rampant in the young nation, even though that spirit was destined to be sorely tried by hardships beyond the wildest

imagination of anyone in that party. One of the seven journals kept by members of the party mentioned that when the expedition first set out, the dog was considered man's best friend. Even after they had penetrated Indian country, for some time the idea of eating their "best friend" was looked upon with revulsion, but by the time they had been on the trip for a year and really found out what hunger meant, the acquisition of forty half-starved dogs as provender became an occasion of considerable jubilation, as well as the source of the contempt some Indian tribes thereafter felt for whites as "dog eaters."

The main plan of action for the Lewis and Clark party had been formulated in Washington from the best available sources – many of which

Lewis and Clark noted these twin basaltic columns, now called the Twin Sisters. They are a feature of Wallula Gap.

proved to be somewhat less than reliable—and in theory was simplicity itself. The Missouri was to be followed to its source in the Shining Mountains (the Rockies). Once over the mountains the party was to follow any river flowing westward, secure in its assumption that any such stream would ultimately lead to the Columbia, the largest stream in the Northwest. The Columbia was to be followed to the sea. Simple as that.

In actual practice, it wasn't quite that easy. Starting from St. Louis on May 14, 1804, it was to be September 23, 1806 before the expedition's odyssey was finished. It took herculean efforts, tremendous courage and ingenuity, a liberal application of military discipline, and more than a little luck before the party reached the headwaters of the westward flowing Clearwater River, followed that beautiful stream into the Snake, and finally, near what is now Burbank, Washington, entered the Columbia.

Compared to the rigors they had endured over the mountains, the rest of the trip was a comparative joyride. The current was swift, the natives friendly, and food relatively plentiful, although the party soon tired of the salmon that formed the basis of the food economy along the Columbia. And when finally, the last rapids had been portaged and they were on the calm lower river, feeling the rise and fall of the ocean tides, their journals grow lyrical describing the beauty of the countryside through which they were paddling. Things haven't changed that much: a person traveling down the Columbia today can feel a blood-brother relationship with Lewis and Clark, for though the Columbia has changed materially in appearance, the basic countryside and landmarks have not, and the river still weaves its magical spell—a spell to which most people willingly succumb.

The beautiful weather of October merged into November, and the party for the first time experienced something that was to become a dreary fact of life: it rains quite a bit on the Pacific Coast. The last leg of the journey was made miserable by an almost constant fog and rain, but finally on November 7, 1805 the mists parted, and there, shining in the distance, was the ocean.

They had reached their goal. The continent had been crossed by land.

The ships, which the Indians had assured Capt. Meriwether Lewis annually visited the mouth of the Columbia, never arrived, so the party spent a miserably wet winter at a makeshift fort built of split cedar planks. They named it Fort Clatsop. Plagued by spoiled and insufficient food, smoky and inefficient fireplaces, hyperactive fleas, and a leaky roof that afforded only nominal shelter from the torrential coastal rains, Fort Clatsop was nobody's favorite place, even though it had the distinction of being the first place in the present state of Oregon to be inhabited for any considerable length of time by white men. Even though they were well aware of the perils ahead of them on the return journey, it was with a joyful heart that, on March 23, 1806, the intrepid band turned their faces eastward, toward home and a warm welcome at St. Louis.

The journey of Lewis and Clark was to have a tremendous impact on the future of the Northwest, for it not only showed the feasibility of overland migration but also established a very solid claim to the new territory for the United States. This was an official exploration mission captained by commissioned officers of the United States Army and conceived with the idea of finding out what country lay between the Rocky Mountains and the Pacific Ocean, up till then unexplored country. The journals kept by the party constituted a very thorough record of the fauna and flora, the geology, a report on the Indian tribes, and a shrewd assessment of the possibilities for development of the country. Their observations, in line with the scientific knowledge of the day, were generally accurate. The journey stands in the annals of human endeavor as one of the greatest and most successful adventures of all time.

A journey of a thousand miles begins with but a single step, and the Lewis and Clark expedition was undoubtedly one of the first steps in a journey that led to eventual American domination of the Pacific Northwest. Before their epic voyage, this whole area, constituting onetwelfth of the total area of the United States, was an unknown wilderness. Now, the full width of the continent had been traversed and could begin to be understood. The topography of the land was known, and some hint had been given of its vast potential. In the enthusiasm generated by the expedition's report, some idea of the manifest destiny of the United States began to be perceived; Lewis and Clark lighted the lamp that was to guide the way of subsequent pioneers through the wilderness.

It is worthy of note that in both coming into

and going out of the Pacific country, the Columbia was the route used by the expedition. This is only natural, for in a time when roads were nonexistent and Indian trails at best narrow and rocky paths, the rivers were the highways of the times; and the Columbia provided the only water-level opening in a wall of mountains seven hundred miles long. This fact was to become very important three-quarters of a century later, when steel rails began to challenge the river as a means of transportation. What the Lewis and Clark exploration did prove conclusively was that any power that sought exclusive domination of the Northwest must control the Columbia River.

THE RICH FUR TRADE established by Captain Cook was the prime reason for the continued development of the Pacific Northwest, the full potential of which was yet to be discovered and exploited. The fur trade provided an immediate source of vast profit for anyone having the means and the courage to wrest from this wild land the treasures it guarded so zealously.

One of those who dared was a New York financier, John Jacob Astor.

Astor's venture into the Pacific Northwest was almost entirely financial in nature—almost. An immigrant from Germany who had amassed a fortune in the London fur trade, he not only had the acumen and drive of the born businessman, but also the perfervid patriotism of a man who had prospered mightily in his adopted country. If he could advance the cause of the United States, that was fine, especially if in the process he could add a few more millions to his fortune.

Two well-equipped expeditions were organized. One was to go by sea and build a post on the Columbia from which the rich fur trade could be better exploited. The other was to travel overland, establish lines of communications, and by personal contact funnel trade to the new post. The overland party was under the command of Wilson Price Hunt, a partner in the company, and consisted of sixty-four men, forty of whom were voyageurs.

Not nearly enough has been written about the voyageurs, for next to the mountain men they were the most colorful characters to grace the pages of Northwest history. Mostly French-Canadians, many of them of mixed blood, they were as carefree and roisterous a crew as ever ran a rapids, shrugged off hardship with a grin, or wakened the echoes of unnamed mountains with a rollicking song. The more dour Americans or British often looked askance at the easy manner in which the voyageurs adapted to Indian ways and considered them lazy and unambitious. Yet these men were as much at home in the wilderness as the Indians themselves. From their homes in Quebec and Ontario, they regularly crossed the wilderness to the Rocky Mountains, establishing a network of canoe trails that served the needs of men who traveled light and were superbly well adapted to living off the land. The Americans may have considered them lazy, but they regularly entrusted themselves to the skill of these men, for the voyageur was probably the best riverman the world has ever produced. Practically amphibious, these men would shoot with laughing nonchalance white-water rapids around which the more pragmatic Anglo-Saxons would have laboriously portaged. But whenever they tied red kerchiefs around their heads and the ubiquitous boating song was stilled, it was time to get somewhat anxious. The red kerchief was for visibility in the churning white water, and whenever a voyageur donned it, one could be certain that the water ahead was anything but placid. Practically all of the major rapids of the Columbia were first tried by voyageurs, for these men would attempt even rapids shunned by the Indians living next to them.

The voyageurs generally got along much better with the Indians than did the Americans, probably because many of them themselves had Indian blood, but more probably because the Indians realized that these men constituted no threat to their way of life. They were hunters and trappers, not colonists. They enthusiastically took Indian wives—something that the Americans did only with varying degrees of reluctance—and the tawny beauty still apparent in some of the oldest families of the Pacific Northwest is evidence that the blend was highly successful. Their undisputed ability as guides and trappers made them indispensable to the success of any fur-trapping enterprise.

The voyageurs ranged the whole West, and the history of the region is replete with the evidence of their travels. Names such as Coeur d'Alene, Pend Oreille, and Grand Teton not only prove that theirs were the first white eyes ever to behold many of the wonders of the West but also reflect a certain Gallic joie de vivre sadly missing in their more serious American and British counterparts.

Astor himself was a fine leader, but when it came to delegating authority, he showed a singular ineptitude. The sea party sailed from New York on September 10, 1810 in the ten-gun ship *Tonquin* under the command of Capt. Jonathan Thorn. Whether Thorn was actually insane or just acted that way has never been definitely established, but his attempts to impose a harsh naval discipline on a motley collection of clerks, businessmen, and voyageurs completely unamenable to such treatment was, to say the least, an error of judgment. Seven months under the tyranny of this crazed martinet was more than the passengers could ever forget; when he finally landed at the mouth of the Columbia, the seeds of discontent had not only been planted but had already achieved tremendous growth. The loss of eight men, needlessly sacrificed in a stupid attempt to cross the murderous bar in undermanned rowboats, had fostered a fanatical desire on the part of the passengers to put as much distance as possible between themselves and the captain; and he, in turn, wanted nothing so much as to get rid of what he considered a bunch of malingering misfits.

The mutual dislike finally predicted the site of Astoria, the new trading post. So that the matter could be settled quickly, a spot near the river's mouth on a small bay behind Point George was selected, and Thorn, after a few more bitter quarrels, sailed northward to trade with the Indians at Nootka Bay. There, he tried to treat the Indians the same way he had treated the Astorians. An Indian chief he had slapped showed more spirit than they had: he and his men boarded the ship and butchered the captain and crew, with the exception of one wounded sailor who crept into the powder magazine and touched it off. The resulting explosion not only provided the natives with makeshift metal artifacts for years but also effectively removed the Astor party's chance of returning to New York by ship, at least by this one. Twenty-nine men and most of the trade goods were lost, for Thorn, with characteristic petulance, had sailed off without discharging his cargo. It was to mean lean days for the Astorians.

They set to work to clear the selected site. Very few of them had ever before felled a tree with an axe, and these Sitka spruces were trees of a size unlike anything any of them had ever seen before. Even when a scaffolding had been erected around the bell of a tree to a height of twelve feet, there was ample room for four axemen to work on the same tree. It was a comedy of errors compounded by the fear all felt that a hostile Indian was lurking behind every bush: they had not yet learned that the Indians of the Pacific Coast were generally not nearly as warlike as their befeathered cousins of the plains — unless provoked by the likes of Captain Thorn.

It was definitely a "learn as you earn" program, because when one of these monsters actually got cut through, it was strictly a matter of chance where it would fall. And quite a few of them didn't fall at all. The forest was so dense and the axemen so inept that more often than not the cut tree would hang up until the key tree could be cut. Then the whole mess would come crashing down, creating conditions so hazardous that eventually at least three men were wounded, one by an explosion of gunpowder used to remove stumps, which also made a stump of his arm.

The work was slow and arduous, but before it was half finished, Astoria welcomed its first white guest. It is doubtful that it ever welcomed a more distinguished one, for the man who stepped out of the canoe flying the British flag on July 15, 1811 was David Thompson of the Northwest Company — and he was several months late.

Short, broad shouldered, and with tremendous physical strength and stamina, he was the epitome of what a fur trader should be — and seldom was. Arriving from his native England into Canada at age fourteen he joined the Northwest Company, a venture of Montreal fur traders who had taken on the formidable task of challenging the Hudson's Bay Company's monopoly. A man gifted not only with a keen intelligence but also with practical good sense, he became the Northwest Company's best cartographer, explorer, and good-will emissary to the Indians. Surprisingly enough, in view of the customs of the time, he founded his many posts, consummated his many deals, and made his many friendships without the dubious aid of the rum which every other trader considered as essential as trade goods. That was one lubricant he could do without, and any post he commanded must necessarily do likewise, for he would not tolerate alcohol on the premises.

Maybe that was one reason the many stellar observations he made with a battered brass sextant, which he carried for twenty-eight years, were so remarkably accurate. Thompson was the first white man to follow the Columbia from its source to its mouth, and also to chart vast areas that were to remain wilderness for many years after he first set his pioneering foot therein.

Thompson was a deeply religious man who often read his Bible around the campfire to his half-Chippewa wife and the voyageurs of his fur brigade, first in English, then in highly unorthodox French, then in more fluent Indian. Widely known to them as the "star man," he was universally welcomed and tolerated. Even the tough Northwest trappers respected his views, strange as they must have seemed to them, for he was certainly the most effective fur trader ever to work the Northwest. A firm believer in the dignity of man, white or Indian, he kept his word, treated everyone fairly, and never asked anyone to do a task he would not himself undertake. The Northwest has produced many notable men but few of the caliber of David Thompson.

Thompson had planned to establish a post for the Northwest Company at the mouth of the Columbia and from there extend the trade of the company throughout the whole Columbia country. High snows in the Rockies had forced him to winter near Lake Windermere on the Columbia, and that particular decision cost him the precious months it took the Astorians to begin their post. When Thompson stepped ashore to be royally entertained by his former companions of the Northwest Company, the Stars and Stripes were already flying from a pole where Thompson would have flown the Union Jack.

This raises an interesting point. The Astorians were, first and foremost, fur traders dedicated to making a profit for themselves and their company. Just as Astor's motives were primarily commercial and only secondarily political, so these men were more interested in aggrandizing their personal fortunes than furthering their country's interests. Their first loyalty was to themselves, their second to their company, and any political advantage that might accrue to their country from their actions rated a distant third. Still, in a confrontation between countries, it was almost a subconscious urge for them to put foremost the interests of their own country, especially when those interests coincided with their own.

There was, however, one small problem. Most of the Astorians, former Northwesterners, were Canadians and therefore British subjects.

Fur trading had a long and honorable tradition in Canada. Endowed with a cold climate, a population that easily took to the ways of the woods, less arable land than the United States, and laws that encouraged a commerce in furs, Canada along with Russia was the prime supplier of furs to the world. There was a ready reservoir of skilled trappers and the necessary collection-and-distribution network, which could be easily expanded on demand. Small wonder that most of the trappers in the Northwest, until circumstances forced the United States to develop its own force, were Canadians.

The men at Astoria, with a few exceptions, were veterans of the Northwest Company. So, when Thompson began telling them at great length what terrible trapping country lay to the east, and how anyone setting up posts in such a poor land was doomed to failure, they took his stories at somewhat less than face value. Thompson's honesty was legendary, but it did not extend to shop talk among equals. He was talking to old trappers who knew the rules of the game and who knew that he, better than most, also knew those same rules: he had instituted many of them.

Preparations were accordingly made to explore the interior country and set up posts as soon as the fort at Astoria could be completed. At the rate the work was going, that could be years. Nevertheless, when Thompson returned upstream, a party of Astorians went with him in two large oceangoing canoes, which Thompson soon outdistanced. They followed in his wake, occasionally reading the proclamations he had posted claiming the whole territory for His Britannic Majesty by right of discovery.

The party followed the Columbia to its junction with the Okanogan, where a small driftwood post was established. A clerk, Alexander Ross, was left in charge there while the rest of the party ranged as far north as the Fraser and Thompson rivers. Ross was without white company for 188 days, whiling away his time by learning the native languages and becoming a remarkably astute trader: he exchanged gewgaws costing 35 pounds sterling for furs worth 2,225 pounds sterling at Canton—not an unreasonable ratio for the times, but nevertheless very good trading.

It was a good thing for the company that someone was minding the store, for trade at Astoria was daily becoming more difficult. The Indians were beginning to realize the value of their furs and were demanding increasingly higher prices. The dominant Chinooks imposed their traditional trade monopoly by forcing the tribes to the north and east to deal with them, rather than directly with the white men. Then, too, the fate of the *Tonquin* became known, and the white men quickly lost the myth of invincibility they had worked so hard to foster. Work on the fort was speeded up as the Indians daily became more hostile. Some Indians who remained friendly passed the word that an attack was imminent.

The Astoria commander, Duncan McDougal, forestalled them with a bluff that was to have serious consequences in years to come. To the assembled Indian chiefs, he showed a small stoppered bottle and informed them that this contained the "spirit of smallpox." If they persisted in their hostility, he would uncork it. Terrified, for smallpox was almost always fatal to Indians, they withdrew. In later years, whenever an Indian died of smallpox, it was felt that some white medicine man had uncorked his smallpox bottle, a belief that was to have tragic consequences and profoundly alter the history of the Northwest.

McDougal had bought a little time, and he used that time to push construction of the fort. With constant practice, the raw beginners had become reasonably hardened pioneers; at least they could now predict with occasional accuracy when a cut tree would fall. They settled down to finish the fort and to await the arrival of the long overdue land party.

The overland party was supposed to have made the trip in one year. It was to be seventeen months before the first ragged, starving survivor staggered into Fort Astoria. In spite of its finely equipped and supposedly experienced personnel, the party suffered nothing but misfortune after it had sought an easier route than the one pioneered by Lewis and Clark and wandered into the terrible Snake River Country. Experienced woodsmen were as helpless as tenderfeet in a land of barren volcanic wastes, where even the few Indians who knew the country intimately were notoriously scrawny. The party had split up, the better to find a viable route, and had discovered among other things that the Snake and its tributaries richly de-

served the name the voyageurs had bestowed: "La Maudite Rivière Enragé" (the Accursed Mad River). The trip over the Blue Mountains took a heavy toll, and it was a sadly depleted and dispirited group that finally arrived at Fort Astoria. Nevertheless, they were reinforcements of a sort, and welcome.

They found the fort in good condition and finally completed. The population was now over a hundred—large enough to discourage Indian hostility—and the arrival of the trade ship *Beaver* in May, with thirty-six more men and an ample supply of trade goods, put the enterprise on a firm basis.

The first American bastion on the West Coast was finally established.

Everything seemed to favor the venture. The Chinook monopoly had been broken and trade in beaver and otter skins was brisk. In June a party of sixty men was dispatched up river, where they established a post near the present site of Spokane and so began to tap the resources of the Inland Empire. Fort Okanogan was still exchanging colored beads for prime beaver plews—that is, semicured skins—and McDougal at Astoria had taken the daughter of the one-eyed chief of the Chinooks, Comcomly, to wife. Washington Irving, who apparently disapproved of miscegenation, reported that this was accomplished only after the somewhat unctuous princess had been subjected to so many thorough ablutions to remove the fishiness common to her tribe that she was undoubtedly "the cleanest Chinook bride ever led to a marriage bed."

So, peace reigned on the Lower Columbia.

Peace may have reigned on the Lower Columbia, elsewhere, it was the War of 1812. To a company of such mixed allegiance as that of Astoria, this presented many personal dilemmas. Most of the Astorians were British subjects working for an American company. The vast majority were Northwesterners and still had lingering ties to their old employer, and out of this situation was born one of the most debated decisions in the region's history. In June 1813 a fleet of Northwestern Company canoes swept down the Columbia to Astoria. Though technically enemies, they were well received by their former comrades. Rather than take the fort by force of arms—a chancy and unnecessarily risky maneuver—they proposed to buy it from the Astorians. Each side had arguments in its favor. The British were in no hurry, because they knew a British sloop of war was on its way to Astoria to take it as a prize. The Astorians, through McDougal's new wife, controlled the food supply at Astoria, and the British had to depend on the fort for protection from the Indians, the fort commandant's new relatives. "McDougal's Maneuver" began to make solid sense.

The Astorians knew that if they sold out, it would be at a tremendous loss, because their opponents knew that it was only a matter of time before the fort became a prize of war. The deciding factor probably was that if the fort were captured by the man-of-war, its proceeds would be divided among the crew as prize money, and the Northwesterners would be frozen out. And so one of the most peculiar and disputed transactions in the Northwest was proposed: a transaction between civilians of two powers at war, designed to cheat one of those powers of the fruits of victory, and negotiated under pressure from a primitive tribe that held both of the negotiators in its power because it controlled the food supply—but which also would be the ultimate loser if no accord were reached.

The Northwesterners still stalled. Pressed for time, McDougal precipitated matters by locking them out of the fort, cutting off their food supply, and pointing his stubby cannon at their massed canoes with lighted matches ready. The time had come, he said, to make a meaningful offer.

The startled British got down to business, and by nightfall, Astoria and its furs had been bought for $40,000—about a third of their true value. Jobs were promised to anyone caring to switch allegiance, and to all others, a safe passage back to New York. McDougal was retained as Factor, then all hands drank numerous toasts to the new regime.

Two weeks later on November 30, 1813, *H.M.S. Racoon*, Capt. W. Black commanding, hove into view prepared to accept the surrender of the American fort or batter it into kindling with its heavy guns. The captain dreamed of glory, his crew of prize money. Those dreams were never to be realized. When they breached the bar and sailed in prepared for battle, they found the fort in the hands of civilians—British civilians at that! Nevertheless, with naval thoroughness Captain Black went through the formality of raising the British flag, renaming Astoria "Fort George," and claiming it for the British Crown. That, in effect, turned out to be a mistake, for he raised a legitimate doubt to the validity of the title the Northwestern Company held to the fort.

One of the provisions of the treaty of Ghent, signed in 1815, reads: "All territory, places and possessions whatsoever taken by either party from the other during the war shall be restored without delay." That included Astoria, since it had been "seized" by a representative of His Britannic Majesty and claimed in his name.

There was to be a four-year delay before that clause was implemented and the fort returned to American jurisdiction, but all it amounted to was running down one flag and running up another. Astor declined to pursue his right in Fort Astoria. His $40,000 had already been invested in some cow pastures in mid-Manhattan and promised to make a better return there than in the fur business. The Northwestern Company admitted American jurisdiction, resumed control, and business continued as usual.

In 1821 the Northwestern Company was absorbed by the Hudson's Bay Company. The union ushered in the heyday of the fur traders, lasted for twenty-five years, and yielded only to the era of American immigration. The Hudson's Bay Company was a trade colossus, with ample resources and the men willing to implement its policies. It was a company that for over 150 years had helped dictate the course of empire and had never failed, in peace or war, to earn fat dividends for its investors. This new entry into the field of Northwest politics was nothing if not formidable.

American historians, especially the early writers still imbued with the hostility engendered by two wars, usually take an unnecessarily unfavorable view of the Hudson's Bay Company and the part it played in Northwest history. That it was a spearhead of British imperialism is generally conceded, even by its staunchest supporters. But instead of being a case of "trade follows the flag," the flag followed the trade the Company helped initiate. And they weren't beginners in the fur trade. They wrote the book on it.

As soon as the Hudson's Bay Company had acquired the assets of the Northwest Company, it sent out its own men to make an assay of what the firm had bought, evidently being somewhat suspicious of the altruism of the new employees, the former Northwesterners. One of the

first and most meaningful decisions was to move the center of operations for the Pacific from Astoria to a more central spot. And thus the Vancouver era was ushered in.

There has been some speculation that the Bay officials named their new headquarters to bolster the claims of Captain Vancouver that he, and not Robert Gray, deserved credit for the discovery of the Columbia River. Be that as it may, the spot they chose, near the junction of the Willamette, was magnificent. Situated on a light rise well above the reach of the spring floods, it commanded a sweeping view of the River, the lower valley of the Willamette, and towering Mount Hood. Surrounded by magnificent trees and dappled natural meadows, Vancouver was the choice site in hundreds of miles of river frontage, and the changes man wrought around it only helped to enhance its own natural beauty. Game of all kinds abounded, the river teemed with fish, and it was soon discovered that the land surrounding the fort was so fertile that very little effort was needed to raise all the fruit and vegetables needed not only by the fort, but also for all its dependents. The fort was bordered with flower beds, which in spring became a veritable riot of color, and its spacious meadows supported herds of sheep and cattle so that there was never a dearth of fresh meat. Fort Vancouver never once knew a day without a full larder.

The fort itself boasted a spaciousness in keeping with the size of the enterprise it represented. An enclosure of 750 by 500 feet, surrounded by a palisade 20 feet high, it had several cannon mounted in corner bastions. These cannons were never to be once fired in anger, though many a welcoming salute roared from their iron throats. All in all, Vancouver was a very peaceful post. It was almost completely self-supporting, with its own workshops, storehouses, and chapels. The houses of the officials, all made of wood, were inside the walls, as was the centrally located mansion of the Factor, but the people who worked at the fort lived in houses grouped outside the palisade. The style of life at Fort Vancouver, as attested by the journals of those fortunate enough to sample its hospitality, was legendary.

Mount Hood towers over the Columbia and Hood rivers.

When it comes to pomp and panoply, few nations can surpass the British. Long experience in dealing with primitive tribes had taught the officials of the Hudson's Bay Company what had the best effect on them, and at Vancouver all this experience was put to work. Ships from Europe could anchor right outside the fort, so the supplies of the world were available to the garrison. Vancouver boasted the best of everything, as befitted the satrapy of a mighty empire. A high-ranking or honored visitor would be met by a six-foot-tall bagpiper in full kilt and ceremoniously piped to his place at the table, which was set with the finest linen, crystal, and china. Although the Factor did not himself customarily indulge in alcoholic beverages, the fort boasted a fine cellar for those who did, and many a bottle of noble wine was consumed around the table. The Great Hall, where distinguished visitors were entertained, boasted a cuisine that would have done credit to Whitehall, and probably exceeded it in variety. All around was a wilderness, but Fort Vancouver was an oasis in a social desert.

In simple justice, it should be pointed out that outstanding as Fort Vancouver was, it only reflected the greatness of the man who for twenty-two years dominated it and the affairs of the Northwest. Physically, mentally, and morally, Dr. John McLoughlin was so outstanding that he has rightfully been described as the greatest man in Oregon history. Journal after journal, historical fact after historical fact attest that here was a trueborn prince of men. Six feet four inches in height, his expressive face crowned by a shock of snow-white hair, this kind though tough and businesslike autocrat was the Chief Factor at Vancouver from 1824 to 1846, and few events in the Northwest during that time escaped the stamp of his personality. Without Dr. McLoughlin, history would have been much different, and only a very few highly prejudiced and bigoted detractors who sought to raise themselves by pulling down a man of greater stature have ever claimed that it would have been better without his ameliorating influence.

During his reign—for that is the best way his tenure could be described—the Northwest was at peace under the laws of the Hudson's Bay Company as administered by Dr. McLoughlin. So well were those laws observed that even the remote back trails were comparatively safe. "The White Headed Eagle," as the Indians described him, was a man who doled out justice impartially to white man or red; and while his judgment was stern and swift, it also was tempered with understanding and compassion. Even to this day, legends among the Indians about Dr. McLaughlin attest that they never had a better friend among the white men, and to this can be attributed the fact that during his years in power relations between the white men and red reached a peak of amity they were never again to attain.

This, of course, was highly conducive to a good trade climate, and it is no wonder that this was the heyday of the fur trade in the Pacific Northwest. And this, in spite of the fact that Dr. McLoughlin was working for a cold-blooded organization often cited as being a merciless behemoth that would not hesitate to sacrifice the lives of hundreds of natives—or anyone else—who stood in the way of making its usual monumental profits. It is only logical to assume that McLoughlin's many deviations from strict company rules were tolerated only because posts under his command invariably yielded excellent returns, and in London that was the ultimate yardstick against which success was measured.

In all fairness to the Hudson's Bay Company, it should be pointed out that the harsh judgments of the firm and its policies came usually from early American observers, who were anything but impartial. As was common in that era, they were usually men of very narrow education, hard working, fanatically dedicated—and with tunnel vision. Bigotry and intolerance masqueraded as "patriotism" or "Christian devotion" and any view other than their own was castigated in the most scurrilous terms. Men of such undoubted energy and ability as Henry Spalding and W. H. Gray unhesitatingly accepted the hospitality and help of the Hudson's Bay Company—as exemplified by Dr. McLoughlin—and then, with a bigotry matched only by their ingratitude, castigated the Company in the most bitter terms and sought to demean even the courteous hospitality of its Chief Factor, who had received them in friendship but who was not of their country or creed. As stated before, it was a measure of the times, and those standards made the conduct of Dr. McLoughlin, who treated all men—whether red or white, Protestant or Catholic, Spanish, French, American, or British—with equal generosity and courtesy, all the more outstanding. Though not an aristocrat, he was in the truest sense of the word a gentleman.

This was the man who was to head the British interests during that political peculiarity known as the Joint Occupancy. This was a compromise settlement—and a reasonably effective one—for a seemingly insolvable set of circumstances. Ownership of the Oregon Territory, an area stretching northward from the ambiguous line marking the Spanish claims in California to a similarly nebulous edge of the Russian claims in Alaska, and from the crest of the Rockies to the sea, was open to considerable question. The Spaniards claimed it by reason of the discoveries of Juan de Fuca and Bruno Heceta. The Russians claimed it by reason of Vitus Bering's voyage, and the fact that the imperious Alexander Baranof had effectively ruled an established fur empire at Sitka long before the British settlement at Vancouver. The British claims stemmed from Vancouver's expedition, which, they pointed out, was an official government voyage, and from the pioneering expeditions of David Thompson and Alexander MacKenzie. The Americans laid claim to the territory on the basis of Gray's discovery, the voyage of Lewis and Clark, a government enterprise, and also on the somewhat tenuous claim that it was a contiguous part of the country ceded to them by the Louisiana Purchase and the Spanish treaty of 1819. Largely left unsaid but exerting covert influence was the popular feeling in the United States that possession of the Oregon Territory was part of the country's manifest destiny.

Spanish claims were not pressed too vigorously. The former mistress of the New World was now only a shadow of her original might, and even those vestiges of her influence were being challenged by her colonies in Central and South America who were tasting the heady wine of independence. What remained of her vitality was too involved with hanging onto the few threads left of her empire to be engrossed with any new weaving. Russia was in a similar position. Already the winds of political unrest were beginning to blow, and her huge domains in European Russia and Siberia absorbed whatever efforts were being made to colonize and settle new lands.

That left Great Britain and the United States. Both were in an expansionist period: Great Britain in building her mighty "empire on which the sun never set" and the United States in developing a huge, raw young country that seemingly would occupy her energy for centuries. But the impetus of empire building was so strong that during this period almost any habitable spot on earth would have been coveted, and the Oregon Country was one of the more desirable spots still available. Both countries wanted it, but neither needed it badly enough to risk a war over it.

Out of this dilemma, Joint Occupancy, first implemented in 1818, was born as a workable expedient. Under its terms, citizens of either country would be given equal rights for a period of ten years. At the end of that time, the situation would be reviewed.

Two things soon became obvious under this arrangement. The first was that no effective legal system could be instituted as long as ultimate sovereignty was in doubt. The second was that sovereignty would ultimately accrue to whichever country settled the most people and thus tipped the balance of power.

The net result of the Joint Occupancy Treaty, which was twice extended, was virtually to leave the Hudson's Bay Company in effective control of the country, and this it exercised with typical thoroughness and efficiency. Without a shred of real legal authority, it enforced a set of regulations based on British common law, common usage, and common sense—and hanged a few murderers who dared question its authority. The company had the only functioning communications system, mercantile establishments, and authority backed with muscle. It simply filled, with the only existing authority, a void that would have otherwise degenerated into anarchy.

The British, who were primarily traders, had aims for the Northwest very different from those of the Americans who soon flooded in, lured by the stories of fertile acres and a mild climate in the Willamette Valley. The Hudson's Bay Company wanted to keep the Northwest in its pristine state: as a vast hunting and trapping preserve from which it could eternally draw an inexhaustible supply of furs. The only colonies it visualized were trading posts that would have a minimum effect on the land. The Americans, on the other hand, being mostly from a rural background, saw in this fertile new country farms, towns, cities, and even states that would someday join the Pacific to the Atlantic across a united country.

All this was to be in the future. The experience of the Hunt party had dramatically illustrated that travel across the continent, a large part of which was a hostile, untracked wilderness, was no picnic. Before families could face that trip with any hope of success, some better, safer route must be found.

The fur brigades made trips from the Rockies to Fort Vancouver. From their posts on the upper reaches of the Columbia and its tributaries, the voyageurs would load their high-prowed bateaux and canoes with huge bales of furs accumulated during the previous year's trading and, voicing the exuberant, lilting songs that were an everyday part of their lives, nonchalantly shoot the white-water rapids of the Great River to bring their furs to Fort Vancouver, where they would be loaded on oceangoing vessels for shipment to London. For security as well as companionship, the contingents from several posts would often travel together. This was a time of great merriment: old friendships were renewed, new friendships were made, and occasionally a few were terminated by flashing knives or gunfire. These small discussions were usually resolved before the arrival at Fort Vancouver, for the "White Headed Eagle" looked askance at such goings-on, especially if they affected the smooth-running operation he supervised.

The many rapids in the river below Death Rapids were usually run, with the exception of Kettle Falls, Celilo, and Cascades, although even these last two were sometimes run during unusually high water. Superb boatmen though the voyageurs were, it was not unusual to lose a canoe now and then, and the most dangerous rapids were littered with the bones of those who had gambled against the might of the River and lost.

Voyageurs and hardened outdoorsmen, traveling light and accustomed to the rigors of the outdoor life, are one thing. Women and children laden down with all the impedimenta necessary to starting a new life in a strange land are another. Still, it was only a matter of time before someone tried.

It must be remembered that not every American was in favor of settling the Northwest and adding its territory to the Union, especially if that meant another armed confrontation with Great Britain. No less a statesman than Daniel Webster was violently opposed to it, calling the country "worthless desert" and fulminating against any bill that might further its acquisition. Southern senators were generally against it, because they saw it entering the Union as an antislavery state. But it had its advocates, some of the most eloquent of whom had never seen the place. These people lectured, exhorted, and made such pests of themselves that at least if Oregon were not well known, it was well discussed. Such a one was Hall Jackson Kelley.

Like someone who falls in love with a picture, Kelley had never seen Oregon. Nonetheless, for at least ten years he extolled its beauty in the most extravagant phrases. To anyone who would listen, he preached the doctrine of manifest destiny—that Oregon must become American territory. No claim was too extravagant, no argument too fatuous for this strangely obsessed man. At last, having made a few converts, he set out for Oregon—by way of Mexico. Meeting his followers at New Orleans, he was promptly robbed by them. Undeterred, he raised another stake and walked across most of Mexico, carrying a huge bag of trade goods for the Indians. He sailed from San Blas to San Diego and, recruiting a strange assortment of hangers-on, headed overland for the Northwest. One of his followers was Ewing Young, who later became a major cattle raiser in the Willamette Valley. But at this stage of the game, Mr. Young left California under somewhat of a cloud. It was rumored that some of his bills of sale for his horses and cattle were home-made, a charge of which he was later acquitted by an American jury.

This information reached Dr. McLoughlin at Fort Vancouver before Kelley got there in October, a sick man and destitute. Always hospitable, in spite of the bad reports he had received about this group, Dr. McLoughlin cared for him but denied him a seat at the gentlemen's table in the Great Hall and thereby earned Kelley's undying enmity. Himself a gentleman, McLoughlin had no desire to associate socially with those arriving in the company of horse thieves. He did, however, personally arrange passage for the destitute and strangely sick crusader back to his native Boston. A stream of pamphlets detailing the beauty of Oregon (from first-hand observations, this time), the perfidy of the Hudson's Bay Company, and the indignities heaped upon him by its Chief Factor followed. Reading one of these today, one is convinced that these are the ravings of a mentally sick fanatic, but they did have some positive results. At least they kept the name of Oregon in the public mind.

Not all of the men who came to Oregon were sick. Nathaniel Jarvis Wyeth, although he was one of Kelley's converts, was a tough, pragmatic Boston businessman of considerable ability. He was, however, a complete tenderfoot, as were most of his associates. Probably not knowing what he was up against, he decided to challenge the Hudson's Bay Company in the fur business. Voyageurs, on hearing of this, collapsed with fits of laughter.

Dr. McLoughlin received Wyeth hospitably at Fort Vancouver, wined him and dined him, and smothered him with personal kindness. He also ruthlessly undercut his prices and imposed a secondary boycott: anyone who traded with the American could not ever again buy from or sell to the Hudson's Bay Company. Faced with this kind of overwhelming competition (which, apparently he completely understood), Wyeth turned to another source of revenue. He thought he might make money by preserving salmon, since this was one venture his friend Dr. McLoughlin didn't oppose and since the ships leaving Fort Vancouver afforded a ready market. He soon found out why there was no opposition. The Chinook method of drying fish worked fine for the Columbia River climate and for a limited time. But transported through a tropical climate over a period of six months, the fish became a rotten, odoriferous mess that didn't exactly enhance his reputation. Maybe that's what gave him the idea that was to make him a millionaire. He sold out the two small posts he had established to his good friend, Dr. McLoughlin, and returned to Boston where he made his million shipping ice to the tropics. It is some measure of Dr. McLoughlin's personality that although he ruthlessly ruined Wyeth's business on the Columbia they remained good personal friends, and the latter always spoke of his erstwhile business competitor in the most cordial terms. After all, business is business and has nothing to do with friendship.

One of the men who came to Oregon with Wyeth was Jason Lee, and with him, the era of the missionaries began. But first, a little background.

IN 1832 FOUR INDIANS appeared at St. Louis. Three were Nez Percé, and one a Flathead, and theirs was a strange mission. They had traveled a thousand miles to seek the white man's "Book of Life." They were courteously received by Gen. William Clark, an old friend of the Indians who well remembered the many services rendered him by the Nez Percé on his famous expedition to the Pacific with Meriwether Lewis. Modern historians generally agree that the Indians were seeking some "big medicine" that would give them the secret of the white man's power and technology, especially that of firearms and gunpowder. In the context of the times, that seems reasonable enough. Their request in 1832 was quickly seized upon by missionaries as a request for spiritual instruction in the white man's religion; the "Book of Life" quickly became "The Book of Heaven," and missionary fever spread throughout the land. The Indians had undoubtedly been exposed to Christianity as far back as the Lewis and Clark sojourn among the Nez Percé. David Thompson, a very devout man, had moved among them, as had Jedediah Smith, who was not only a first-class mountain man but also a practicing Christian. Then, too, the voyageurs, practically all Catholics, had brought a widespread knowledge of Christianity to the Indians. In their minds, it was only natural to believe that the white man's technological superiority stemmed from his "Good Book," which must be strong medicine indeed if it could help him achieve his wonders. Therefore, to possess the "Good Book" would give them the secrets of firearms and gunpowder.

Somehow, it didn't work out that way. Something must have gotten lost in the translation, for what the Indians got was a host of eager missionaries intent on making them good Congregationalists, Presbyterians, Methodists, and Catholics, something they viewed with little or no enthusiasm. The first of these missionaries was Jason Lee.

The Reverend Mr. Lee had been received at Fort Vancouver with Dr. McLoughlin's usual courtesy and been royally entertained by him. In the talks that followed, the Factor had easily persuaded Lee that the proper place to set up his mission was south of the Columbia River, in the valley of the Willamette. Quite aside from the fact that here were the best lands, it also suited the Hudson's Bay Company policy of diverting all American settlers to the lands south of the River. Everyone knew that Joint Occupancy was only a temporary measure and some day a line of demarcation must be drawn. Most people expected the line to be the Columbia River, with the lands south of it to become American territory, while the north bank would be British. Since the new settlers trickling into the region were mostly Americans, Dr. McLoughlin advised them to settle south of the River, so that when the line was officially drawn, they would be in the United States territory.

Unlike some of his more straitlaced successors, Lee, a Methodist, was quite well accepted by the pioneers and mountain men. He realized that any changes he could make among the Indians and pioneer settlers of the Willamette Valley would have to be done gradually, and because of his tolerance of certain local practices which he personally abhorred, he was more successful than some of his more impatient brethren who were to follow him.

It did not take Lee long to realize that the Indians were a lost cause, spiritually speaking. Their way of life simply did not jibe with his teachings, and they could see no valid reason for a change. So, he easily rationalized his mission to be among the white settlers in the Willamette Valley, only eighty-six of whom were Americans.

Lee's activities in the Willamette Valley soon became more secular than spiritual. A firm believer in manifest destiny, as befitted a disciple of Hall Jackson Kelley, he preached his doctrine to the people already there so effectively that when he returned to Washington in 1838, he took with him a petition signed by twenty-seven Americans and nine French-Canadians asking Congress to officially abrogate the Joint Occupancy Treaty and annex Oregon to the Union as a state.

Congress wasn't impressed, but the American Board of Commissioners for Foreign Missions was. It voted $42,000 to further the work of the Western missions, and under its aegis twenty-one American men and their families traveled to Oregon. None was a fur trapper. The complexion of immigration into Oregon was changing; and it was further changed in 1842 when 107 people crossed the plains in the first large wagon train to Oregon.

These were true pioneers, and they were blazing new trails. It is one thing to move a party of hardy voyageurs on horseback or in canoes across a wilderness: it is quite another to move men, women, and children in clumsy covered wagons over an area completely devoid of roads. The early stretches of the pioneer road to Oregon were littered with abandoned bulky furniture—often family treasures—as the grim realities of wilderness travel rapidly transformed tenderfeet into hardened pioneers with a completely altered set of material values.

Strangely enough, that first wagon train made it through the wilderness much more easily than did some that were to follow. And the next year, 1843—the year of the Great Migration—900 Americans in 120 wagons lumbered into The Dalles, the end of the Old Oregon Trail.

This presented somewhat of a dilemma to Dr. McLoughlin. The policy of the Hudson's Bay Company was to discourage immigration, especially Americans, to the Oregon Country. He had already been severely criticized in London for his generosity to previous settlers, and now here were 900 people, almost totally destitute, camped on his doorstep. The situation would not wait for an opinion from London. Dr. McLoughlin, in apparent defiance of Company orders but in accordance with his own personal creed, ordered bateaux to go up to The Dalles and help the pioneers in any way possible. It was a decision that was to cost him his job but earn him a place not only in Oregon history, but also in the hearts of the more decent people to whom he was extending the hand of friendship in time of need.

Dr. McLoughlin loaned the hungry and mostly broke settlers seed grain and cattle. To those who could pay, he sold supplies. To the many who could not, he offered jobs, and in some special cases furnished whatever was needed at his own expense. Whether he was moved by altruism or a pragmatic assessment of the situation, the net result was the same. The American domination of the Oregon Country through settlement became an accomplished fact. Had he allowed the new pioneers to starve, as some of his hardheaded Hudson's Bay associates advised, he might have had blood on his hands—and not necessarily American blood only. Starving men, especially Americans toughened by six months of frontier rigors and with guns in their hands, did not view those who decreed starvation with any degree of affection, and it is entirely possible that a small but bloody war for possession of the Oregon Country could have broken out then and there.

The pioneer groups had already demonstrated that overland access to Oregon was possible, and where the prairie schooners had rolled, so could United States Army cannon. McLoughlin was not only a man of peace but also an eminently practical man who could read the writing on the wall. The future of the Oregon Country was to be as an American state and not as a British hunting preserve.

The decision had not yet been finalized but soon was. Precipitated by the death of Ewing Young, whose large estate could not be legally distributed because there were no established legal channels, a meeting was convened at Champoeg, on the banks of the Willamette. Officially known as a "wolf meeting" whose avowed purpose was the control of predators, it soon developed distinctly political overtones. The Americans, led by mountain man Joe Meek, proposed a provisional government modeled after that of the United States. The vote generally followed national lines, with Americans for, and Hudson's Bay men, who were mostly Canadians, against. At the last minute, two French-Canadians changed their votes to the American side, and the provisional government was adopted, 52–50.

The government authority was entirely self-delegated, but the Americans drew up a code of law "until such time as the authority of the United States is extended to us." It generally followed the model of the United States Constitution and was antislavery, but also markedly anti-Negro, probably a reflection of the large number of Southerners among the settlers.

And so the control of the region effectively fell to the Americans, especially since the wagon train of 1844 added almost three thousand Americans to the Oregon Territory, an overwhelming majority, and marked a transition from fur-trading to agriculture as the dominant industry. It was still to be a few years, and turbulent years at that, before the state was admitted to the Union in 1859, but by the treaty of

Ione Town Park, on the Coeur d'Alene River, which is one of the large tributaries of the Upper Columbia.

33

1846 the forty-ninth parallel was extended to the ocean as the northern boundary of the United States, and all of Oregon as well as present-day Washington became American soil.

The Hudson's Bay Company policy of concentrating American settlement south of the Columbia River had been largely successful, but in spite of its best efforts, some Americans had settled north of the River, notably at Fort Nisqually and at Tumwater, near Puget Sound. There were, however, over one thousand Canadian and British nationals in the same area. Some retained their allegiances, but most of those who stayed became American citizens. In any event, the problem, if indeed it were a problem, settled itself in time. Children born in the newly American territory were Americans by birth, and many of them were to become prominent in the affairs of the state of Washington when it finally was admitted to the Union in 1889.

Dr. McLoughlin was one of those who opted for American citizenship. His career in the Hudson's Bay Company ended in 1846, largely as the result of the generosity he had shown American settlers in defiance of company orders. He was forced to pay personally for the supplies he had advanced to the settlers, many of whom conveniently chose to ignore the debt. This and the ingratitude and intolerance he encountered in his retirement at Oregon City tarnished what should have been his well-earned golden years. Largely on the fact that he had not been a citizen when his claim was filed, a factor conveniently ignored in other similar cases, his choice lots in Oregon City were claim-jumped by a Methodist minister whom he had previously befriended. While this injustice was belatedly rectified, many historians have claimed that he died embittered and impoverished.

He certainly had reason to be embittered, but recent research has indicated that he was anything but impoverished. His estate was valued at $172,000, a sizable fortune on the frontier; and no man had a better claim to fortune and the good things it supposedly brings than did the "White Headed Eagle." The state of Oregon honors him as one of its founding fathers, but the best tribute of all, and the one he would have most sincerely appreciated, is the respect that succeeding generations have paid him. This man, through the exercise of his magnanimity, shaped the destiny of the Northwest and carved for himself a unique place in its annals.

The Columbia River country certainly has no dearth of magnanimous characters. In fact, it is replete with them, and high on that list would be Marcus and Narcissa Whitman, whose lifetime work was crowned by martyrdom at the hands of the Indians they had so earnestly and unsuccessfully sought to convert. Of all the people who helped establish American dominance in the Northwest, few have captured the imagination as has this remarkable couple. Their story, especially as embellished by their co-workers, who were among the first chroniclers of the Northwest, has become surrounded by such a maze of fables and romanticized fancy that their acknowledged accomplishments have taken an undeserved secondary place. That is a pity, for the unvarnished truth is a solid basis for the adulation in which they are held.

Marcus Whitman, M.D., was commissioned by the American Board of Foreign Missions to scout the Columbia River country with a view of establishing a mission there. Traveling with a group of trappers working for the American Fur Company, he saw mountain men for the first time at their rendezvous at Green River. The sight both appalled and fascinated him, for Whitman was a complex blend of hearty, vigorous outdoorsman who could feel empathy for these half-wild men, and zealous, temperate Congregationalist who found their riotous drinking and wenching on a jarring collision course with his own staid beliefs. Yes, he concluded, the Columbia country would be a fertile field for a mission, especially if its inhabitants lived up to the samples he had seen at Green River.

Whitman was to become a fast friend of many of these men in the next few years, and the good relations he generally enjoyed with them had much to do with the success he enjoyed in establishing the Oregon Trail. His stock improved considerably in their eyes when he expertly removed a three-inch-long arrowhead some Blackfoot had embedded in Jim Bridger's well-muscled back some three years before. The young doctor, they figured, was a good man to have around even if his views on liquor and sex were downright peculiar.

Whitman returned to New York and convinced the Mission Board that an Oregon mission was not only feasible, but practically mandatory if the Lord's work were to be done. He also was introduced to Narcissa Prentiss, a young schooteacher who had written the board of her desire to aid in any way possible the conversion of the heathen. What better way than as the wife of a doctor who was already headed for the mission fields? No matter that they hardly knew each other: the Lord's work must be done. And so, what was a matter of convenience became a basis for marriage and, in light of what was to follow, a very valid and solid one.

The young couple traveled on their honeymoon, almost all the way across the continent. The other members of the party, recruited only with some difficulty, were the Rev. Henry H. Spalding, his wife Eliza, W. H. Gray (the secular manager of the party), and two Nez Percé Indians.

It was an oddly assorted group. Dr. Whitman, although sharing the narrow views endemic to the times and his education, was apparently more tolerant than Spalding or Gray, both of whom were so violently partisan in their views that the books they subsequently wrote have been largely accepted only as points of departure. Their views on Britishers, Catholics, the Hudson's Bay Company, or anyone even slightly disagreeing with them are so biased as to be largely discounted. Yet, these were sincere, hard-working, extremely talented men who were to have a large role in the future of the Columbia River country.

The wives were as different from each other as were the men. Narcissa Whitman had a good general education, was comely, buxom, and golden haired, with a beautiful singing voice and a sunny disposition. Often accused of being aloof, she was in fact as selective of her company as the frontier allowed. The selection available was somewhat narrow, which may have explained her reserve. Her journal reflects a keen intelligence, good observation, and deeply felt emotion. In every way, the almost accidental mating with Marcus Whitman proved to be a very compatible match.

Mrs. Spalding was dark, coarse featured, and enjoyed fragile health—all the way across the continent. That she was able to find reservoirs of the necessary strength when it was needed says much about the character of this indomitable woman. Her relations with her dour husband were occasionally stormy, especially when she reminded herself that Spalding had once asked Narcissa's hand in marriage and been rejected. The jealousy and ill will engendered by this was largely responsible for the establishment of separate missions, although this was to prove a mixed blessing, for while it

diluted the combined strength of the party, it also spread the efforts of the missionaries over a wider area.

Mrs. Spalding's role in the Northwest missions has frequently been downgraded, especially in comparison with her more glamorous coworker, Mrs. Whitman. In fact, she was probably the best educated of the four, with several classical languages at her command and a gift for Indian tongues in which she quickly became fluent. Through her linguistic ability and the influence she soon held over the Indians, the Spalding mission was to be the most successful Protestant mission in the Northwest.

The trip cross-country was comparatively uneventful. Whitman had intended to show that travel across the continent was possible by wagon, and to that effect he had driven a light wagon as far as Fort Boise with no more trouble than he would have had on a New York State country road. There, the Hudson's Bay people, who evidently realized the import of the vehicle, persuaded him to leave it, while the party continued on horseback, the ladies demurely riding side saddle. The Indians, accustomed to seeing their young girls astride, thought the position ridiculous, as indeed it was.

The mission party reached the Hudson's Bay post at Fort Walla Walla in September and proceeded by bateaux to Fort Vancouver, where Dr. McLoughlin received them in his usual baronial manner. Having two white women as guests, especially one as pretty and radiant as Mrs. Whitman, was quite an occasion at Fort Vancouver, and the hospitality, as Mrs. Whitman's letters put it, "was endless and most kind."

Narcissa Whitman's radiance was no accident. Somewhere between Angelica, New York, and St. Louis, the marriage of convenience had suddenly blazed, and Marcus and Narcissa Whitman found themselves deeply, humanly in love. The change was evident in both of them: they laughed joyously, seemed not to notice hardships, and publicly showed their affection, much to the disapproval of the straitlaced Reverend Spalding, who claimed such a display was most unseemly, but who probably was remembering that Narcissa had turned down his offer of marriage and was now recklessly happy with another man. That jealousy was to color their relationship for the rest of their lives and have a most unlikely side effect: it was responsible for the establishment

of a relatively successful mission among the Nez Percé.

Narcissa Whitman's and Eliza Spalding's place in history is secured by many of the events of their lives, but the fact for which they are most often remembered is that they were the first white women to travel from the East Coast to the Oregon Country. Up till then, it had been deemed impossible, but Marcus Whitman had proven that it could be done. The Indian women, of course, had been doing it from time immemorial, but they were considered different. They didn't ride in wagons. Narcissa Whitman and Eliza Spalding had, and where they could go, others could follow. This journey had proven that anyone who was willing could get to Oregon by the overland route, and with little more discomfort than was common in traveling the horrendous roads of the populated East. It was only a matter of time till this message sank in, and the western flow of population to the Columbia River country began.

The two white women stayed at Fort Vancouver as honored guests of Dr. McLoughlin while the two men reconnoitered their new mission sites. On advice of the Factor, who pointed out that the Willamette Valley was already served by the Methodist mission at Chemeketa, Whitman established his mission in the beautiful and fertile Walla Walla Valley at Wailatpu, the "Place of the Rye Grass." This was Cayuse country, and while this tribe undeniably had always been suspicious of the whites, Whitman considered it the best possible site for his new venture. Spalding, on the other hand, chose his site at Lapwai, in Nez Percé country about 110 miles from Whitman's mission. Each man hoped that distance would solve their problems.

It did not. Each meeting between the two men degenerated into arguments and continued ill will.

It should be mentioned that diverse personalities were involved. Whitman was much the more likable character: gregarious, friendly, adaptable, highly religious, but more tolerant, a man of tremendous drive and ability. Yet his eleven years at Wailatpu were to yield him only eleven converts. Spalding, for all his conten-

tious nature, narrowness of mind and bigotry, produced a far higher ratio of converts, even though he personally was liked by few people, especially whites, who met him. He did, however, have a better understanding of Indian psychology. This may have been one of the reasons Whitman was the prime target of the subsequent massacre, and not Spalding.

The constant bickering between the two factions was reflected in reports to the Mission Board, whose answer was to order both missions to be closed. Whitman was aghast, especially since he and Spalding had patched up their differences and were enjoying a temporary truce. With characteristic impetuosity, he chose to ride back to the Mission Board headquarters in Boston to plead his case, leaving on October 3, 1842.

Many of the earlier historians have given as Whitman's reason for making this ride of over fifteen hundred miles in the dead of winter the fact that he wanted to "save Oregon for the Union." Several books on this subject have been written, but modern research does not bear this out. Whitman wanted to save his mission and the years of hard work he had put into it. He knew, of course, that with increased American immigration into the Oregon Country, the balance of power was being tipped in their favor. He also knew that if Oregon became American, his mission work would be greatly facilitated since he would be working among friends and in his own country. And deep down in his heart, he undoubtedly wanted this beautiful country of which he had become so fond to become part of his native land. So while the principal motivation was to save his job, it was probably a combination of reasons that prompted his decision to set forth on that fateful trip.

The rigors of the trip were such as to challenge a Kit Carson or a Jim Bridger, but Whitman, a superb outdoorsman, felt himself equal to the gamble. And he won! His epic ride across the wilderness in the dead of winter is the stuff of which Hollywood epics are made, but to him it simply was a way of getting to the seat of power with his side of the story—that the missions should be preserved.

Whitman reached St. Louis around March 3, 1843, but instead of proceding directly to Mission headquarters, he detoured to Washington. There, he spoke with influential friends in the government, no doubt detailing the glories of the Oregon Country and its hoped-for ultimate destiny. He only stayed two days, so that

PREVIOUS PAGE. *Dry Falls State Park. Here, at the end of the last Ice Age, a cataract forty times larger than Niagara thundered over the cliffs.*

obviously was not his prime destination. He spent most of his time at Mission headquarters in Boston, where he received a very chilly reception for having left his post without authorization. Whitman, however, was a very determined man who certainly had not crossed the continent just to be lionized at tea parties and be told his mission was to be closed. Marshaling his most persuasive arguments, and with considerable editorial support, he convinced the Mission Board that the two missions should not only be retained, but even expanded.

The train for the Great Migration of 1843 was being formed, and Whitman offered his services, which were gratefully accepted. Although not the leader of the train, as he has often been portrayed, he was certainly a tower of strength and a man whose counsel was sought and heeded, for he was familiar with the trail, and his credentials as an outdoorsman were impeccable.

Whitman was to have four more years at Wailatpu during which time it was to become one of the most prosperous and well-stocked stations on the Oregon Trail. The wagon trains made it a regular port of call, for here was a microcosm set in the wilderness, run by a man who knew the problems of pioneers. Narcissa daily taught school to Indians and half-breed children, many of them sons and daughters of her friends, the mountain men.

The Cayuses had proven to be poor bets as subjects for conversion, as had most of the tribes except the Nez Percé. They were also disturbed by the increasing flow of white men who were encroaching on their lands and bringing diseases to which they had no inherent immunity. Smallpox, for instance, was a temporary inconvenience to the whites, while with the Indians, who had no built-in genetic resistance, it was tantamount to a death sentence. The Cayuses noticed that the whites Dr. Whitman had treated for measles all recovered, while the red men died. Surely, they thought, the white medicine man makes good medicine for his own people, and bad for the Indians. According to their code, such a medicine man must die.

Whitman was aware of the building hostility, but certainly was not ready on November 27, 1847, when the Indians attacked. The Whitman dream ended in two days of murder, rape, and looting, during which Marcus and Narcissa Whitman were butchered by the Indians, along with eleven men. Two children died from sickness and exposure. Five men, eight women, and thirty-four children were taken captive, to be ransomed a month later by Peter Skeen Odgen under orders from the Hudson's Bay Company.

The Indian Wars that followed lasted till the Great Treaty of 1855 supposedly ended them. Actually, they continued sporadically for several more years, effectively slowing down immigration to the Columbia River country, and sowed the seeds of discord that continue to this very day.

Eventually, the war drums throbbed no longer, the wagon trains resumed, and a new era unfolded, the era of modern development.

Undeniably, it was a colorful era: a time made lustrous by the deeds of brave men and women whose plans required "time and distance," as Marcus Whitman put it. Looking over the vista of the years, it is evident that this lovely corner of the United States is what it is because there were people who dared to dream and then with hard work made those dreams come true. Without people like Robert Gray, David Thompson, John McLoughlin, Jason Lee, and Marcus and Narcissa Whitman, its story might have been much different, and not nearly as inspiring, for each of these people left an indelible mark on the pages of time and on the country by which the Columbia flows on its way to the eternal sea.

The River Rises

DAVID THOMPSON, the Northwest Company's famous "star man," was puzzled. In his capacity as explorer, cartographer, and fur trader, he had tramped over more of the Pacific Northwest than any other white man, and if anyone knew about regional rivers, he was that man. But here was a stream that didn't fit the usual pattern. Rivers on the west side of the Great Divide invariably flowed in a westerly direction, but here was one going almost due north, toward the Arctic Ocean, rather than toward the Pacific as any decent Northwest river should. And this wasn't just any river, either! Fed by streams cascading off the steep mountains on either side, it was growing larger by the mile and already, only a hundred miles from its source, was carrying a volume of water that stamped it as a major river.

That wasn't the only peculiarity of this stream. Its headwaters were only a mile or so from the Kootenay, which the Indians told him emptied into this stream about a hundred miles away. Yet here the Kootenay was already a good sized navigable river, while the "main stream" at this point was only a few feet wide.

The rugged Selkirk Mountains, as seen from Rogers Pass on Transcanada 1.

David Thompson was the first white man to find out what many after him were to corroborate. The Columbia is an unusual river and doesn't always follow the ordinary rules.

Standing at the headwaters of a great river engenders a feeling unlike that produced by any other part of that stream, however beautiful it may be. This is the source, the beginning, and everything else that is to come springs from here. That feeling certainly swept over me that hot July day while I gratefully shed my travel-stained clothes and plunged into the crystal clear, cold depths of Columbia Lake. Drinking a cool draught of that water was a symbolic gesture, for here at the headwaters I was completing a journey that had started at Astoria in February and would still take the better part of a year before I had seen the complete length of this beautiful stream. It is very seldom that a writer can as completely immerse himself in his subject as I did that day, and the memory of the emotions engendered there have persisted throughout the whole project and helped me immeasurably in my determination to pass on to others the sights, feelings, and emotions this majestic river evokes so freely.

It is only fitting that the Columbia, one of the world's most spectacular streams, should have an aquamarine gem of a lake as its headwaters. A glacial trench bulldozed by the glaciers of the last Ice Age, it is flanked on one side by the granitic heights of the Rocky Mountains and on the other by the more wooded slopes of the Selkirks, from whose heights icy mountain streams feed the lake. The southern edge of the lake, choked with sedges, shelves off to a smooth plain extending to the nearby Kootenay. On this plain is the town of Canal Flats and that historic peculiarity, the Waillie-Grohman Canal, better known locally as Grohman's Ditch.

Canal Flats looks something like a set left over from an old Western movie, and Grohman's Ditch could have been part of it. As early as 1807, the ubiquitous David Thompson had portaged from the Kootenay to Columbia Lake, a distance of some six thousand feet, so the fact that only a short distance separated the Columbia from one of its major tributaries was well known. This must have intrigued other men before W. A. Waillie-Grohman conceived the idea of connecting the Kootenay and the Columbia, for the name Canal Flats antedates his venture.

He was, however, the first to do anything more than just talk about it.

Waillie-Grohman owned extensive holdings in bottom lands at Creston. The lands were fertile and eminently suited for orchards except for one thing: periodically, the Kootenay flooded and buried his newly planted orchards under a layer of silt.

A canal at Canal Flats, he reasoned, would play a dual rule. It would siphon excess flood waters into the less densely populated Columbia River valley and furnish a water link between the two river systems at a time when the paddlewheel steamer was the main form of transportation. A London syndicate, lured by promises of 300 acres of land for every $2,500 invested in the project, furnished the backing, and in 1890 Chinese laborers with wheelbarrow, pick, and shovel were hacking out a ditch 6,700 feet long, 45 feet wide, and 4 feet deep. The canal boasted a single 100-foot lock, which was judged to be ample to handle any boat seeking passage.

Apparently, the canal was all too successful in draining off the spring floods on the Kootenay. The floods were transferred to the valley of the Columbia, which by this time was rapidly filling up with settlers, till litigation and counterlitigation effectively tied up operation of the canal. The flood waters, however, still poured through the ditch till irate farmers took matters into their own hands and built a dam across the canal, thereby effectively stopping both drainage and navigation.

There wasn't that much navigation, in an era of railroad building, and by the time the canal was operational so were the railroads. With their greater flexibility, they proved to be formidable competitors to the steamboats. Demand for passage through the canal was somewhat less than overwhelming: only two steamers made the passage, and one of them only after a judiciously placed charge of dynamite had demolished the dam. Waillie-Grohman sadly gave up the project that had taken up so much of his energy and other people's money.

Portions of the canal are still visible today. Choked with vegetation and consisting mostly of stagnant pools, it is a wildlife preserve par excellence, which is probably quite commendable but hardly what its promoter had originally intended. It did, however, make a point. It had proven that it was definitely possible to join the

Kootenay and the Columbia, and in so doing, had effectively made an island of the Selkirk Range, an area larger than England. In recent years, the reopening of the canal as a flood-control measure has been proposed, but it is doubtful if such a project will ever get beyond the talking stage: the valley between Canal Flats and Golden is today as densely populated as is the area to be afforded flood relief.

The fledgling river flowing in a northerly direction from Columbia Lake is about twenty feet wide at the lake outlet, but its growth is rapid. Steep mountains, most of them snow-capped the greater part of the year, feed a multitude of creeks into the young river which at this point meanders through a pleasant, fertile valley with rich meadows and snug, well-kept homes.

A dozen miles or so from Columbia Lake, the River widens into the first of the river-lakes, Lake Windermere. This is beautiful boating water, in a setting of stunning majesty, but there are numerous dead trees in the water with the tops barely covered, suggesting not only that the boater had best mind where he is going, but also that the lake has not always been at its present level. A community beach, well used by those from the pretty little lakeside town of Windermere, indicates that the people hereabouts are aware of the recreational advantages the River offers and make good use of it.

For the next hundred miles, the Columbia loafs through a flat, extremely fertile green valley, a country very reminiscent of the Thames country of England, were it not for the mountains towering on either side. The River is lazy, dropping only four inches to the mile, and would have hardly any current at all but for the press of new water constantly entering the river and swelling its flood. While the water is probably biologically clean, in spite of the cattle grazing in the river banks, it is often milky grey, especially during the spring and summer runoff, for this water is glacial in origin and carries a large load of suspended rock-flour. The region downstream from Columbia Lake is often called "the Channel," and sometimes that channel is hard to find, since the River splits into numerous sloughs which, because of the lack of current in the main river, are often indistinguishable from the main stream.

It really doesn't make much difference, on a lazy summer day, especially if time isn't too pressing, which channel the prow of one's kayak enters, because the country is all beautiful and the boating can only be described as idyllic. The banks are tree covered, good campsites abound, and any straight stretch of the river reveals a vista of field, river, and mountain breathtaking in its perfection.

The only town of any size on this stretch of the Columbia is Golden, where the wild Kicking Horse River thunders into the main stream, almost doubling its flow. Golden is a pleasant little city with some very nice, cooperative people. It also has some good sporting goods stores where the customers don't mind telling you how to fish for the big ones and are free with their information about the river conditions downstream. It never dawned on us to doubt this information; everyone was so helpful and interested in our projected trip down the River to Mica that we were sure we were getting the best local help available. So we bought the tackle they recommended and set off downstream, blithely confident that the trip to Mica was nothing but a pleasant milkrun.

Fifteen miles north of Golden, at Donald Station, the road leaves the river, which flows now quite swiftly between heavily wooded banks. I got most intimately acquainted with this particular stretch of river, along with my bowman, Don Hodel, who when he wasn't shooting white-water rivers or skiing, bossed an outfit known as the Bonneville Power Administration as administrator. I figured anyone tough enough to take all the flack tossed at the head of such an organization would be an ideal companion for a ten-day cruise through the most remote country still left on the Columbia. Having put in supplies for the trip to Mica Dam at Golden, we were there advised by a supposedly reliable source that the River below Donald Station was all placid water, the backwaters of Mica Dam. So, when a few miles below Donald Station the current began to run more swiftly, we just counted our blessings. We were in a seventeen-foot Klepper two-place kayak equipped with a rudder, an extremely sturdy and maneuverable craft, and because it was raining, a stormcover covered the cockpit to keep out the water. That was fortunate, for around a sharp bend in the river, we heard a low, muted rumble, the river suddenly slanted downward, and we were in rushing white water.

The Columbia is famous for this. On this

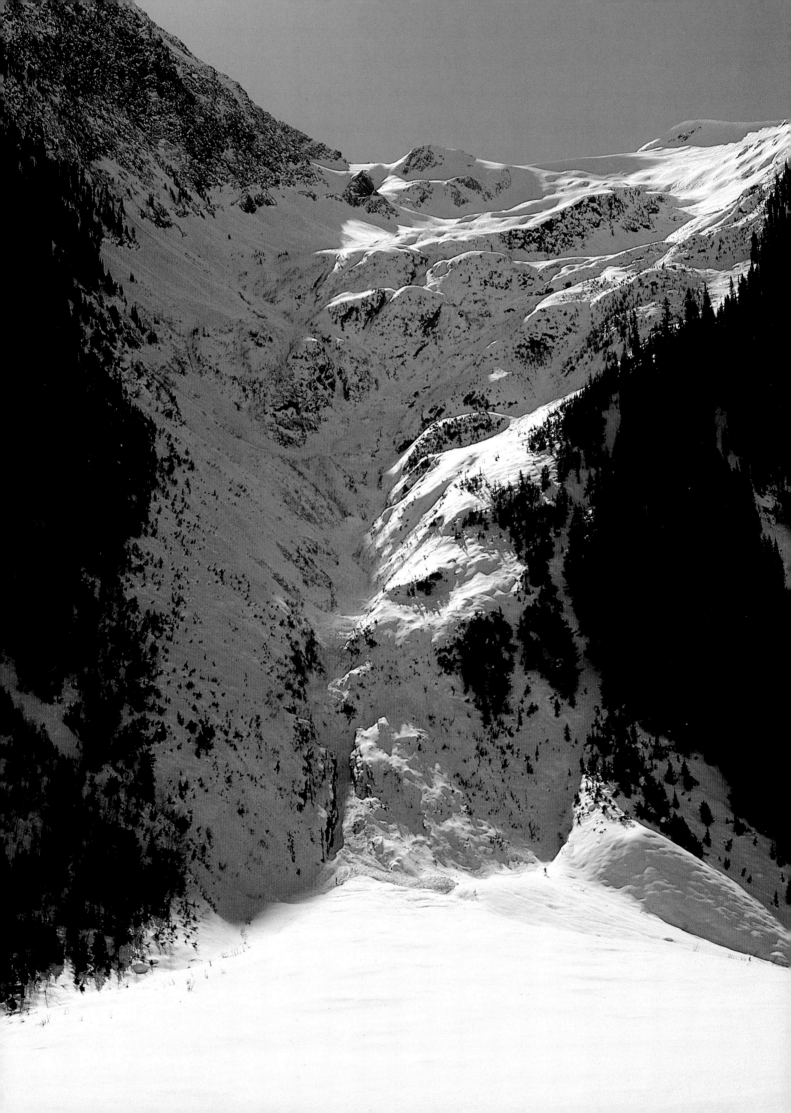

Centuries of accumulated snows compress into glacial ice and ponderously creep down the Selkirk Mountains near Rogers Pass.

upper reach of the River the voyageurs had encountered what they called Surprise Rapids, so named because they gave no notice of their presence until you were in them with no place to go except downriver. According to our map, Surprise Rapids was buried under Mica Reservoir, but if we weren't there, this stretch of the River was suddenly putting on a very good imitation.

THIS WAS OUR FIRST experience with the wild Columbia River. Until then, we had been happily cruising on placid waters and enjoying the superb scenery in spite of the rain; but now the River surged with a deep, ominous power that let us know that all those stories we had heard about the Columbia's awesome strength had considerable basis in fact. Soon we were drenched in spray, and in spite of the best maneuvering I could manage, huge waves broke over our bow and slammed us around like puppets on a string. Our only hope was to ride it out and pray as we paddled, for the walls of the River had suddenly become dark, dripping cliffs, with no possible landing place. To make matters worse, the Columbia had nar-

rowed to half its original width, and huge wet rocks scattered here and there thrust their shiny surfaces upward, sometimes only inches above the foaming waters. The River twisted and turned through a tortuous canyon, creating large whirlpools that every once in a while would disgorge a twenty-foot log as effortlessly as a matchstick. That it could likewise swallow a seventeen-foot kayak if given a chance we didn't doubt one bit, but if we had anything to say about it, that wasn't about to happen.

No one was saying anything anyway, since words would have been lost in the terrific roar of the water. Don was actually getting the worst of it, since any wave that broke over the prow (and in spite of the best I could do on the rudder, many of them did) would have to sweep over him before it hit me. He was taking the beating; all I was doing, besides worrying, paddling, praying, and steering, was getting very, very wet.

There seemed to be no end to the rapids. As fast as we got out of one, there was another only ten yards ahead. Fortunately, we had maneuvered our way into the center of the river, where

Water released from the bottom of Mica Dam is under such pressure it throws head-sized boulders over two hundred yards.

the water was swiftest, but also where there were fewer of the rocks that offered the greatest danger. Capsizing in that water would have been somewhat unpleasant, although I doubt we could have gotten much wetter.

Both Don and I are experienced white-water men and had the greatest confidence in our sturdy craft, which had taken us through very rough waters on other rivers. We also had unbounded confidence in each other and spontaneously acted together like a well-drilled team, and that makes a pretty good combination. Although we had never before been in water of quite this tremendous, boiling power, we must have simultaneously noticed that we were taking the toughest the River could throw at us and were coming out on top—which, on this or any other river, is the only place to be. And so it was that after that first five minutes or so of acute apprehension, exhilaration began to replace anxiety. Not completely, but at least the spark was there.

And then, just as we thought the worst was over, the canyon shouldered in, and the River seemed to stand on edge. The current carried us directly toward a towering cliff, at the base of which a huge rock, ten feet or so from shore, cleft the water and poured it like a millrace through a narrow opening. To the left of the rock, a huge whirlpool sucked debris into its whirling maw with a remorseless ease that bode no good. I chose the millrace, right down the vee formed by the deflection from the wall and the eddy from the whirlpool.

Waves kicked out from the wall and bounced off our stormcover. Huge, boiling crosscurrents tugged at our craft and tossed us about until I began to wonder if it were any use at all to paddle so frantically and work that rudder like fury. We missed the rock by at least a foot (Don says three inches) and shot past the edge of the maelstrom into the comparatively calm water of a swift, straightaway rapid.

I think it was then that I really began to appreciate the feeling that must have motivated the fabled voyageurs who first shot the rapids of Donald Canyon. David Thompson graphically describes that huge rock and "monstrous whirlpool, sufficient to swallow a canoe and its cargo without a trace." That canyon had not changed appreciably since the days when red-kerchiefed voyageurs took fur-laden canoes through this same maelstrom. They probably felt the same exhilaration we felt as they pitted their strength

and skill against the River, and probably the same sense of relief when finally, five miles down river, we pulled into the first available inlet and, gasping for breath, gave thanks that our bones hadn't joined the many that litter the bottom of this canyon.

We had covered almost five miles in thirty minutes: pretty slow time in a car, but not bad when you're dodging truck-sized rocks, ten-foot whirlpools, and six-foot waves.

For a few moments neither one of us spoke, then I voiced a thought Don had in mind but couldn't spare enough breath to say: "The first thing I'm going to do when I get back to Golden," I said, "is look up that husky six-footer who told us the river is flat all the way to Mica, and kick the stuffing out of him."

"Save some for me," was his heartfelt answer.

To a couple of river rats who had just survived what we considered a reasonably exciting experience, it should have come as a somewhat deflating thought to find out that Donald Canyon was not considered one of the major rapids on the old, untamed Columbia and was regularly shot with seeming nonchalance by voyageurs familiar with it. The large rock, true, was worthy of mention in their notes, but the rest of it was routine and not even worthy of any special apprehension. Compared to the maelstroms of Surprise, Redgrave Canyon, Kinbasket with its twenty-two miles of white water, or Box Canyon on the Middle Columbia, Donald Canyon is an easy run regularly negotiated during high-water conditions by power-boaters and not to be mentioned in the same breath with the major rapids of the Columbia. Apparently, we had hit it at its worst, and if this one was "easy," running some of the really bad ones must have been a highly interesting proposition. As it was, we ran it at a good time. When Revelstoke Dam drowns out the rapids of Revelstoke Canyon, Donald Canyon will be the only section of the Columbia even faintly reminiscent of what the River used to be before its wild spirit was tamed in chains of steel and concrete. And we had shot it in a kayak! I must confess we had been duly impressed by the power of the untamed river whose name is mentioned with respect whenever stories of white-water boating are recounted.

We had come out of the canyon now, and suddenly the misty rain stopped, and the sun broke through the clouds. We were suddenly floating into a fairyland of shimmering, dripping, green and gold light as the sun broke in slanting rays through the mist-soaked foliage. Hurriedly, I broke out the cameras from their waterproof bags and began shooting. Enough of being a riverman: I was once more a photographer. It was only a brief interlude before the clouds closed in and the rain resumed, but it was enough to show us that this section of the Columbia can be not only deadly but also supremely beautiful. It was almost as though the gods of the Columbia, after having awed us with their power, were now trying to woo us with their beauty. On both counts, they succeeded.

We were now in the headwaters of Mica Reservoir, a huge fifteen-million-acre-feet storage area that holds more water than any other lake on the Columbia River. Over a hundred miles of wilderness separated us from the next outpost of civilization, or so we thought. Then suddenly the air hummed and throbbed to the drumming roar of diesel motors, and high up on the left bank a Canadian Pacific passenger train threaded its way atop a steep cliff. Oh, well, at least the right bank was wilderness.

This was the first time that Mica Reservoir had been filled to capacity, and the surface of the huge lake was dotted with debris that had floated as the water level was raised. Huge trees, brush, and bark, often matted together by the wind into huge windrows, impeded our path and often forced us to thread our way through a seemingly impassable maze of floating islands. It slowed up progress considerably, but it also gave us a chance to appreciate the magnificent scenery through which we were passing. This is the famous Big Bend country, a country as wild today as it was in the day of David Thompson. It is a country alive with the crash of water falling from precipitous cliffs, draining ice fields on perpetually snow-clad mountains. It is a country of hanging glaciers, blue-black forests, and teeming wildlife. It is also the wildest country left on the Columbia River, where the hand of man is yet to be felt. Yet this very reservoir on which we were cruising was raised to its level by the hand of man, and in a few months the waves smashing into a new littoral would begin to reshape the shores. We were seeing it at the right time. The next year it would be different.

The Canadian Pacific and its accompanying access road left us at Beavermouth, a large flow of water from a wide gash in the mountains to our left. Since night was falling, we were looking for a break in the debris lining the shores to make camp for the night. Easier said than done—the edge of the river was lined for miles with floating logs and trash that effectively kept us fifty yards from shore. Finally, the mouth of a creek where the current had kept the floating trash from accumulating gave us access to shore, where we spent a wet but nevertheless restful night in our snug mountain tent.

The Kinbasket Lakes are submerged now under the waters of the reservoir, but once these were the most beautiful spots on the Columbia. Three mountain peaks soaring from the water's edge reach up to over ten thousand feet, their snow-covered heads reflected in a lake of surpassing beauty. Large creeks—really rivers, in point of volume—crash into the lake, and all around is the primeval forest. Fifteen million acre-feet of drinking water! In a day when pollution is a major problem and most of the world's surface water unfit to drink, it was really something to be able to reach over the side of the kayak and dip up our drinking water from the lake on which we were cruising.

The lake is not always placid. A thin line in the distance, a raggedness along the smooth horizon, was our first warning. We had been warned that the reservoir was capable of sudden and violent storms, and since we were near the center of the two-mile-wide lake to avoid the masses of debris, we headed for the west bank as fast as we could. By the time we got there, the squall hit us. In a matter of minutes, we were breasting three-foot waves.

Trying to worm our way through logs that were bobbing up and down and crashing together wasn't exactly our idea of fun. Neither was it fun to head into waves that were now up to five feet and getting bigger by the minute. The wind was shrieking along in gusts that whipped the tops off the tumbling waves and sent scudding sheets of spray flying into our faces, while the rain, now in sheets, came horizonally on the wings of the wind and stung like storm-driven hail. Our only hope was to run with the wind and take a chance on broaching when we turned: not a very pleasant prospect, expecially when we knew that a storm such as this one would blow us back half a day's travel that we had bought by steady paddling. Still, it was better than swimming.

Just as we were about ready to try this ad-

mittedly risky maneuver, we got one of those lucky breaks that only a beleaguered kayaker could fully appreciate. A large cottonwood had fallen into the lake, and another tree had jammed into it, keeping it at a 45-degree angle to the waves. Into the natural breakwater formed by this, we gratefully pulled in, and spent the next hour bobbing up and down on twelve-inch swells while only thirty feet away, the waves were running a good five feet from crest to trough and tossing good-sized trees around like matchsticks. We found out later that this storm packed sixty-mile winds and caused considerable damage throughout the province of British Columbia; but we actually enjoyed it, having as we did a perfectly safe if somewhat wet grandstand seat.

The storm subsided as quickly as it had arisen, but the swells engendered by it persisted for the rest of the day. That only made the ride more interesting, as we breasted swell after swell, rising and falling in a steady pattern that at least broke the monotony. Soon a helicopter came buzzing over, then turned and flew back when we waved cheerily and pointed downstream, in the direction we were going. I suspect our Royal Canadian Mounted Police friends, who were aware of our presence on the reservoir, may have had a few doubts about our ability to survive a storm of that kind.

Some good-sized rivers join the Columbia: the Bush, where we saw a timber salvage operation and met a couple of the friendliest loggers in British Columbia; the Sullivan; and finally, at the base of towering mountains, the Canoe. Back before the reservoir was formed, this was the roughest stretch of the Columbia, with twenty-two rapids. While not in a class with Redgrave Canyon or Death Rapids, they were still extremely rough water which even the amphibious voyageurs approached with respect. My regard for voyageurs, already quite high, became even higher, and I certainly hoped that my paternal great-grandfather hadn't been just bragging when he told me, when I was still a little boy and he was in his nineties, that his grandfather had been a voyageur, and so some

PREVIOUS PAGE. *The highway between Golden and Revelstoke in British Columbia, is one of the most scenic in the world, as this view of the Selkirk Range will attest.*

of that same blood ran in me. Now, all those rapids are drowned by Mica Reservoir, and some day, when the river is cleared of debris, the mountains will echo to the shattering roar of powerful outboard motors rather than to the song of the voyageurs. Change, it certainly is, but is it progress?

We had not seen a single boat on the reservoir for over fifty miles: strange, for such a beautiful body of water, until you begin to realize that boats coming down from Golden would have to run Donald Canyon, and boats coming up from Mica would have to buck miles of debris: not recommended even for tough fiberglass hulls, and rough on propellers. No, the reservoir was the sole domain of two crazy Americans in a kayak, and we liked it that way.

Until the Columbia reaches the Canoe River it runs almost due north, but here, as though yielding to the pressure of the water pouring into it from the right, the River makes a sharp bend and turns left, thereafter flowing first southerly, and then in a westward direction as Northwest rivers are supposed to do. This is the Big Bend. The River has finally flanked the Selkirk Mountains and is flowing toward its ultimate merger with the Pacific Ocean.

That bend in the river is meaningful. Without it, the Columbia probably would have been, like the Mackenzie, an even larger river than it is. But it would have flowed through a wilderness and emptied into an arctic sea, far from the sight of man. It would not have been the Columbia. Its destiny was shaped here, at Boat Encampment, when it turned south instead of north, and became the Great River of the West, instead of some mighty but comparatively unknown arctic stream.

There was a Hudson's Bay Company post here at Boat Encampment through which most of the fur trade of the Upper Columbia was channeled. From here, the fur brigades made their yearly trip to Fort Vancouver, portaging at Death Rapids, Kettle Falls, and sometimes Celilo and the Cascades. The rest of the rapids were run or lined. I can only symbolically raise my hat in combined respect, admiration, and envy. Now, those were real rivermen!

Mica Reservoir has several lumber operations along its shores, two of which we observed: one at Bush River, the other near Canoe Reach. Much of the timber floated by the rising water is perfectly sound, long-lived cedar that brings a premium price on the lumber market for siding and shakes. So huge is the total amount of wood involved that authorities figure it will take at least twenty-five years before loggers can satisfactorily clear the reservoir, thus not only salvaging a valuable resource, but also clearing the lake so that it can fulfill its potential for recreation and transportation.

Mica Dam is itself worth a trip, if for nothing else, simply to see this, one of the engineering wonders of the world. At Mica Creek, ninety miles north of Revelstoke, the free world's largest earth-filled dam stands 650 feet high and impounds the second largest lake in area on the Columbia River system. An underground powerhouse carved 600 feet deep into living rock houses six huge generators with a combined capacity of 2.5 million kilowatts of electrical energy; it will power and light the far off cities of Calgary, Edmonton, Vancouver, and Victoria. Miles of underground galleries house all the complicated gear it takes to turn the power of falling water into electrical energy. And all this is taking place in an area where less than twenty years ago the hand of man was practically unknown, and where even to this

day bear and deer amble through the streets of Mica Village.

The village is at the terminus of a paved road running eighty-five miles north from Revelstoke. It is a self-sufficient little settlement with most of the social amenities of a much larger town, including a golf course and a curling rink. It is completely dominated by British Columbia Hydro, which runs the dams and distribution system and takes a paternalistic interest in seeing to it that its employees lack for nothing in the wilderness. A more beautiful – or lonely – spot for a village would be hard to imagine, but judging by the happy faces of the inhabitants, loneliness is one thing no one fears in a small town where everyone necessarily knows everyone else.

Even here, or maybe it is especially here, at the beginning of the River, its magic is felt, and the people living by it consider themselves fortunate, for to be touched by its beauty is to experience one of the great emotions this world can provide.

Here, as everywhere, the Columbia casts it spell.

The Upper River

JUST AS IT IS IMPOSSIBLE to fully appreciate the Columbia without having seen its birthplace, so it is necessary to see the country that feeds its growth to understand its character and magnitude. The Columbia is a mountain stream; it is mountain born, mountain fed, and never fully loses its characteristics of an overgrown mountain creek. Fire and ice shaped the mountains from which the Columbia springs. The Canadian Rockies, Selkirks, Cariboos, Bugaboos, Monashees, Kootenays, Cascades, all were born of the titanic upheavals resulting from the pressures of the Earth's internal fires, and were then planed and contoured by crushing masses of ice formed by centuries of sustained snowfall.

The remnants of these glaciers remain to this day, still altering the shapes of the mountains, deepening the valleys, rounding off the peaks, and feeding their icy waters into the Columbia and its tributaries. In the upper reaches of the River, no fewer than five separate mountain ranges chill the moisture-laden clouds blowing in from the Pacific, deposit their burdens as snow, and then release their impri-

The Rocky Mountains tower over the lake impounded by Mica Dam. In the old fur-trading days, this was a very busy part of the River.

soned waters during the summer months. To this fortuitous fact is due the Columbia's unique characteristic of heavy stream flow during the summer months, when other rivers, born in gentle climes, normally flow at a greatly reduced rate.

With the possible exception of the Grand Tetons which, far to the south, are part of the Columbia River drainage by way of the Snake, the Selkirks provide the most spectacular scenery within the River's system. While not as high as the main peaks of the Rockies, they gather more snow and have more glaciers and a greater percentage of the sharp, jagged peaks usually associated with grand mountain scenery. Mount Sir Donald, a smaller counterpart of the Swiss Matterhorn, rises in a spectacular monolith to a height of 10,808 feet. It is a great favorite of mountain climbers, for its perpendicular faces offer not only a stiff challenge but also a solid granite structure that makes climbing a pleasure—both of which features a true mountaineer greatly appreciates. The view from the top is well worth the climb: a spreading panorama of mountains, lakes, and over a hundred glaciers, one of which, the Grand Glacier, covers an area of better than thirty square miles. Drainage from this glacier feeds the Illecillewaet River which richly lives up to its name ("swift flowing"), for this brawling mountain stream drops thirty-five hundred feet in forty-five miles. Engineers seeing this stream automatically reach for their pocket calculators, then gaze in awed disbelief at the total power potential their calculations indicate; but other, probably more poetic souls simply gaze on it with equal awe as it tears its way down rocky canyons as a wild thing of completely untrammeled beauty.

Almost all of the five hundred miles or so of the Columbia that is Canadian spring from the mountains. Below Mica Dam, the River runs swiftly, through a sloping but gently falling valley, so that the River only occasionally shows white water. Glaciated mountains fringe it on either side, and almost every mile of its length, creeks and rivers, some of them draining spectacular hanging glaciers, tumble into the river to add to its already impressive flow. Some of these, such as Downie Creek and Goldstream River, have rather interesting backgrounds.

Anyone viewing Goldstream River from the highway bridge would be justified in believing this river to be completely unnavigable. There are falls fifteen feet in height, and the roar and crash of the waters is so great as to make voice communcations impossible. In 1866 during the heyday of British Columbia's Gold Rush, when gold seemed to be found on every creek in the Cariboo and Selkirk Ranges, these falls were cursingly portaged, and the Goldstream was one of the main arteries into the Selkirks. There are still vestiges of the ancient mine workings, but no appreciable amount of yellow metal is presently produced, although people still try. Gold, which was the magnet that first brought people to this "impassable wilderness," was found in some quantities all through the Cariboos and Selkirks, and some lucky miners who struck it rich laid the foundations for present-day fortunes. Nowadays, however, gold is more apt to be produced as an impurity in the refining of lead and zinc ores—a more prosaic method than prospecting but one of considerably greater reliability.

Four miles above Downie Creek is the famous Death Rapids, the most fearsome spot on the Upper Columbia to the ancient voyageurs. Even these men, who feared neither man nor devil and to whom white water was only a challenge to be laughingly accepted, laboriously portaged their fur-laden bateaux and canoes around this stretch of the Columbia, for those who attempted it invariably disappeared into the monstrous whirlpools of Death Rapids and were never seen again. To get to the rapids, one must leave the road and cut through dense woods to the top of a steep-walled canyon. When the foliage becomes dripping wet with spray and the earth literally trembles with the force of the pounding waters, you're close. The river here is less than a hundred feet wide and cascades over a series of faults, so that the stream is really a series of falls. Only the tremendous volume of the river gives the surface any degree of continuity, and even as it is, there are numerous places in the rapids where the waves are monstrous. It can only be conjectured what they look like from eye level; there are no known eyewitnesses who have survived. The roar of the River is really more a sustained rumble, tremendous in its intensity and power, and can be heard for miles. Even David Thompson feared Death Rapids so much that rather than attempt them or portage four laborious miles around them up the steep cliff, he chose to come down the Kootenay to the Columbia in his epic journey to the sea.

This is the worst spot on the Columbia, and one with a grisly record. During the Gold Rush, when there was considerable traffic on the Upper Columbia, canoes often got caught in the current above Death Rapids and, having no place to land because of the steep canyon walls, were inexorably swept into the maelstrom of swirling waters and crushed like eggshells. The rapids are mercifully short, not over two hundred yards, but are succeeded by another, much longer series of abrupt falls (named Priest Rapids, from the body of a luckless blackrobe fished out of them) that would themselves have a bad reputation were anyone to attempt them. The reputation of the rapids was such that Downie Creek, immediately below them, became the high point of steamboat navigation on the Columbia.

Downie Creek was the place where the pioneering steamboat captain, Leonard White, in 1866 gingerly edged his boat *The Fortynine* into the bank to disgorge eighty-nine fresh, enthusiastic prospectors and pick up a load of more than one hundred broke and discouraged ones. In spite of the numerous IOUs he was compelled to accept, he repeated the process every ten days and paid for his boat in one season, so brisk was the trade and so high were the fees he charged.

The traditional Canoe Race from Downie Creek to Revelstoke was run for the last time in 1976, since thereafter the initial work on the Revelstoke Dam, five miles above the town, made the race impossible. Canoeists from all over the United States and Canada converged on Downie Creek and competed, supposedly for prizes, but actually for the sheer fun of running down forty miles of scenic river that in spots become pretty nasty, and for drinking the sponsor's excellent beer.

Don and I had been having our usual wonderful time, enjoying a milkrun down the Columbia from Mica: smooth, swift-running water, with only enough white water to keep it interesting. Knowing Death Rapids' fearsome reputation, we took our boat out of the water well above them, although reluctantly. The scenery was absolutely superb, with high mountains bisected by forested valleys, down every one of which a stream clattered its way into the Columbia. Surprisingly, we saw more bears than deer and absolutely no people on the river till we reached Downie Creek and its canoeists. We did see a large steel barge which loggers had assembled on the banks of the river to give themselves access to the rich stands of timber on the far side of the river, but we would hardly class that as a recreational vehicle.

We asked about the race. . . . "Sorry," we were told, "canoes only allowed in the Canoe Race, no kayaks."

So we were relegated to the role of spectators and critics as the canoes challenged the rapids in a recreation of the annual pilgrimage of the fur brigades. Some did not make it: they spilled in a stretch just about where the dam will be. Both Don and I agreed it was not nearly as bad as what we'd been through in Donald Canyon. Now, if they'd only let us in that race. . . .

The road from Revelstoke to Mica, eighty-five miles of new asphalt, was built to service Mica Dam and Mica Village. It runs through nearby clearcut forests all the way, for this area has been extensively logged for the last ten years. When the new dam above Revelstoke starts to back up water, it will inundate only stumps. This is superb logging country, with huge stands of virgin cedar and fir, and logging in this area is undeniably the largest industry, as indeed it is in the whole of British Columbia. A high-tension line runs along the edge of the clearcut from Mica into the power grid serving the major Canadian cities in the area. Its steel towers follow the highway most of the way, sometimes striking a jarring note on the countryside, and at other times blending into it as a natural part of the scenery. All the way from Mica the vistas are superb, with one mountain setting blending into the next, each one seemingly more enchanting than the last. With such a plethora of beauty, it seems that the occasional jarring note of the transmission line is acceptable, especially when I realize that what may be a jarring note to me is a symbol of the good life, of employment, of human progress to someone else.

Revelstoke, sitting comfortably on a plain overlooking the Columbia, is surrounded by snowcapped mountains, so it comes naturally by its reputation of being a summer recreation center and a winter mecca for skiers. It sits at the head of the Upper Arrow Lakes on a site not far from the original town of Second Crossing, which is now Revelstoke's "Old Town." The Canadian Pacific Railroad exerts a tremendous influence all through these mountain towns: its coming to Second Crossing was the reason the town grew rapidly as a mercantile and service

A crevasse parts the Columbia Ice Fields. Part of the water from this glacier flows to the Pacific, another part will reach the Atlantic via Hudson's Bay.

center, so what could be more natural than to re-name it after Lord Revelstoke, one of the financiers who made the project possible?

Revelstoke is a pleasant little town with good stores, restaurants, and much-welcomed hotel facilities, although for some reason or other gasoline is higher priced here than anywhere else in the Columbia River system. Its city hall has fresco decorations describing in very lyrical terms the building of the Canadian Pacific which makes fascinating reading and looking, although the picture of Louis Riel, the leader in Canada's little known Civil War, could use a little refurbishing. The city is a jumping off place for several trips, all of them fascinating.

The most popular trip is that on the Transcanada Highway over Rogers Pass to Golden, a spectacular ribbon of asphalt which passes through Glacier National Park and has some of the most breathtaking scenery on the North American continent. The highway borders the pass discovered by Maj. A. B. Rogers, an American who is remembered not only as an ace rail-road surveyor, but also as a purveyor of picturesque profanity such as occurs only once in a century. The major in full cry, it was said, caused foliage to wither, strong men to blanch, and horses to cover their ears with their hooves.

The route he surveyed orginally crossed atop mountains all the way to Golden, but winter avalanches were so costly in lives and property that part of the route was put underground in the five-mile-long Connaught Tunnel. Travelers over Rogers Pass can still see traces of the old roadbed and snow sheds, some of them only partially visible beneath rubble brought down by snow crashing from the heights frowning overhead. There are also the stone skeletons of bridges built high above the creeks, fine examples of the artistry that was often brought to the plebeian task of affording a crossing over a mountain creek for a set of steel rails.

Transcanada One, the nation's major cross-country highway, was dedicated at the top of Rogers Pass, culminating years of road building through virtually impassable county. A memorial arch commemorating this event is set against a background of jagged peaks that form the backbone of the Selkirks. Water from this spot flows eastward into the Columbia, and a hundred feet away, westward, also into the Columbia, for here the two parts of the river, one flowing northerly, the other southerly, are only seventy miles apart. In between is the Selkirk Range, which contributes to the River a sizable portion of its total flow.

Another fascinating trip originating in Revelstoke is westward along Transcanada One to Salmon Arm. This goes through the Monashee Range, which is just now being discovered as excellent skiing terrain, especially for anyone affluent enough to afford helicopter hire. Transported above the timberline to the vast snowfields above, the lucky skier can go for miles in one direction through trackless snow that has never before known the touch of a ski other than his own—and that is any dedicated skier's idea of heaven. The Bagaboos are also famous for this type of skiing and draw an ever-expanding clientele, especially in summer when glacier skiing provides that added fillip of danger that makes any sport more exciting.

Rogers Pass, on Transcanada 1, is one of the most scenic routes in North America.

From Salmon Arm the traveler can continue westward to the bustling city of Kamloops, one of the most rapidly growing cities in British Columbia, and deservedly so, for few cities can offer greater accessibility to outdoor recreation right next to metropolitan amenities. Southward from Salmon Arm through Enderby and Armstrong, the roads lead to Lake Okanagan and its charming trio of cities, Vernon, Kelowna, and Penticton. These three cities sit in British Columbia's interior "banana belt," for although the mountains nearby get enough snow to maintain an outstanding winter sports activity, the valley has a mild climate year-round and grows a great part of Canada's best fruit. Kelowna, midway on Lake Okanagan, hosts a regatta in August that is internationally famous; while Penticton, at the southern end of the lake, boasts the finest fruit in Canada as well as beaches decorated with beautifully filled bikinis.

Penticton is also the center of the wine industry in British Columbia, using grapes grown in the fertile soil of Okanagan Valley. Special hardy varieties of *vinifera* grapes are being developed here that can adapt to local conditions and thrive in the comparatively short growing season. If enthusiasm, hard work, and the application of liberal amounts of hard cash prevail (and they seem to be doing very well), this area may well emerge as the northernmost area in America to produce fine wines. Anyone who has experienced the hospitality and friendliness of these delightful people cannot help but wish them well.

All three cities share a legendary monster, Ogopogo, known since the early days by the Indians, which is Canada's answer to the Loch Ness monster and allegedly dwells in the far depths of Lake Okanagan.

The river flowing from the lake flows southerly through Osoyoos, crosses the United States border (where it is spelled Okanogan), flows past Omak and Okanogan, and joins the Columbia near Brewster. A Washington State Park facility with excellent dioramas commemorates the spot at Fort Okanogan where Alexander Ross first learned that the Indians valued colored beads above beaver skins. It is well worth the slight detour.

While these side trips from Revelstoke are well worth the while, the one on which we will concentrate, since it follows the Columbia, is the one going south to Shelter Bay. And here we first come to the Arrow Lakes, by common consensus the most idyllic spot on the whole Columbia River. The Arrow Lakes, Upper and Lower, are caused by that great glacial action that also dug Okanagan, Slocan, Kootenay, and Chelan. With the Selkirks on the left and the Monashees on the right, they inherit the gift of beauty. They live up richly to this legacy, for this stretch of the Columbia has been noted for its quiet beauty since the days of the first voyageurs. The upper reaches of the Columbia, above Mica, are wilder, the mountains bolder and more spectacular, the streams swifter, but here the grandeur is tempered with gentility, and the beauty is something that the human spirit can assimilate and enjoy. The mountains are less rugged, more rounded and gentle, the banks less precipitous, with occasional shelving beaches that make camping possible and the enjoyment of the whole environment effortless. It's still wild country heavily wooded, but here in its upper stretches a highway runs parallel to the river and the wilderness scenery can be enjoyed while traversing it in comfort.

The Arrow Lakes were so named because of the large number of arrows found protruding from some of the fissures in rocks along their banks, a fact noted not only by the voyageurs, but also by Father Blanchet, an early Jesuit missionary to the Indians who kept a meticulous and well-written journal. He reasoned the arrows many have been part of some ritual in which the Indians indulged as they cruised along the lake shore. Considering the value Indians put on laboriously made or purchased arrow points, that seems to make sense; otherwise, unless protected by a religious taboo, the arrows would surely have been collected for reuse.

The Arrow Lakes are of one level now, backwaters of the British Columbia Hydro Hugh Keenleyside Dam above Robson, but once there was an eight-foot differential, with a narrow strip of river appropriately named The Narrows connecting them. These lakes were the favorite part of the Columbia River for the fur brigades on their way to Fort Vancouver, and their echoes have been wakened by many a rollicking boating song. The lakes are gently flowing, full of fish, and still have on their banks crumbling cabins that show that some of the voyageurs were sufficiently enamored of this region to put down roots and stay awhile. During the era of steamboats on the Columbia, the lakes were great favorites with the captains, affording as they did a welcome respite from the rigors of the river both below and above them. They are still a favorite place for recreationists, but practically unknown and empty, for they extend from Robson to Revelstoke, a distance of almost a hundred miles, and only the upper and lower ten miles show any degree of activity. Unfortunately, this condition cannot last, as the knowledge of this uncrowded paradise will inevitably spread.

The road from Revelstoke to Nakusp is through a complete wilderness. Signs at Nakusp warn, "Next services 104 km." and they mean it. The road is new and has not yet accumulated all the man-made detritus that so often disfigures a highway. Hopefully, the powers that be will recognize that in a completely uncluttered highway, they have a unique and edifying attraction, and will keep it that way, for this road affords unparalleled vistas of the Monashees glittering with snow, girdled with dark belts of timber, and the river gleaming like a silver ribbon between its forested banks.

There is a free ferry at Shelter Bay that carries trucks, cars, and passengers across the three miles or more of open river and affords a spectacular view from the center of the river, where commonly only boaters venture. The view alone would make the crossing memorable.

Nakusp was once a booming steamboating town, but now tourism is its main industry. This was a night layover spot during the steamboat days, and if some of the local stories are to be believed, a decidedly lively one. Now it's a lazy tourist mecca in a setting of surprising beauty, with the broad river at its front door and rounded wooded mountains beyond. Nakusp gained a modern beach and waterfront from the higher water backup by Keenleyside Dam, and it lost a few landmarks long on history but short on appearance.

Highway 6 forks at Nakusp, going either to Slocan or the Narrows, depending on which fork you take. The Slocan fork skirts Slocan Lake, easily one of the most spectacularly set lakes in North America—a long, dark, deep aquamarine body of water, a marine trench bordered by steep cliffs and high wooded banks with only a few alluvial flats on which two silver-born towns, New Denver and Silverton, sit. These towns were the result of fantastically rich silver strikes in the 1890s which brought a flood of prospectors up the Slocan Valley and up the Columbia, then overland from the Arrow Lakes. The ruins of some of these workings stand to this day in the picturesque little towns, which now mine the more durable and richer lode of tourism.

The other fork of Highway 6 from Nakusp also leads to the Narrows Ferry, where the road leaves the River. Since it was my determination to see all parts of the river from source to mouth, my dependable kayak came into use again, for the next sixty miles of the River are inaccessible by road, unless you know your way through a maze of largely overgrown logging roads not usually open to the public.

Cruising the lake by kayak is no hardship, especially if one has an amiable, muscular, six-foot-plus son-in-law to help supply the motive power and companionship. My daughter had the good sense to marry a man with whom I share a mutual respect, understanding, and admiration, which makes for a wonderful relationship, especially when we must share the same small boat. Bruce Gordon is one of those happy, goodnatured big men who loves the outdoors, is at home in it, and doesn't mind doing sometimes more than his share of the work. I couldn't have asked for nicer company.

We made camp one night near a ruined log cabin after we had covered thirty miles without seeing a solitary soul on one of the most beautiful bodies of water either one of us had ever seen. In early September, the temperatures were mild, the lake waters bracingly cool, and the river bank, as it slowly unfolded past the rippling wake of our kayak, a never-ending source of fascinating observation. Here a ruined cabin, showing that someone, long ago, liked this spot well enough to build a home in the wilderness. There a decaying flume where once huge logs had ridden a blanket of water to the lake, there to be formed into rafts and towed to the mill at Robson. The hills bordering the lower Arrow Lakes are rounded, gentle, with a variety of coloring that made them a never-ending kaleidoscope.

Never had the Columbia cast its spell more effectively, for I still look back at that part of the River as the most friendly and enjoyable I have experienced anywhere in its whole length. Those old voyageurs knew what they were taking about when they described this part of the Columbia so lyrically. After all, they, too, had seen the whole River and were entitled to make a valid judgment: a judgment in which I heartily concur.

Bruce enjoyed it as much as I did. Although he hadn't seen the whole Columbia, he was willing to take my word for it, and the fact that he wants to go back there again next year should prove something. We moored the kayak next to a huge cedar log conveniently floating right where we meant to land, quickly pitched camp, and had a cooking fire going.

The day had been overcast and misty, though comfortably mild. But now, a distant rumble heralded a coming storm. We took the precaution of beaching our kayak well beyond the reach of any storm-driven wave and turned in for the night. After paddling thirty miles, we were ready for a good night's sleep.

I was wakened by a monstrous clap of thun-

A sturdy two-man kayak is a wonderful way to get acquainted with the rugged country of the Upper Columbia.

der, seemingly directly overhead. The interior of our mountain tent lit up as though illuminated by a giant flashbulb, and by its light I could see Bruce peacefully sleeping. Crash followed crash, the very ground shook, and the interior of the tent was intermittently bright as day. Bruce still slept. Then came a gently scattered patter of rain which soon swelled to a drumming tattoo as the full fury of the late summer thunderstorm descended on the taut nylon over our heads. Bruce stirred and opened his eyes.

"Hey," he said, "it's raining!"

That was a slight understatement. The summer of 1976 was the wettest in memory on the Upper Columbia, and rain certainly was nothing new to me. Don Hodel and I had four solid days of it on the Mica Reservoir. But this rain came down as though it were being poured out of a cosmic bucket. It is certainly one of the most comforting sounds in existence if one happens to be warm and dry, as we were, but I couldn't help but think how it must have been back in the days of the old fur trappers who

traveled so light that a tent was considered a luxury and who depended on a tightly woven blanket to provide warmth and shelter from the elements.

The next day was also misty, but with that certain softness of light such as is prevalent in the English Lake Country. Across the wide expanse of the River, the Monashees reared their rounded bulk, their heads wreathed in clouds. The River still had a considerable swell from last night's storm, but this soon subsided into a glassy smoothness, broken only by the ripples of our wake as our synchronized paddles flashed in a steady rhythm that smoothly ate up the miles. I highly recommend this as a wonderful way to really see, feel, and understand a great river: it would be difficult to get much closer to it any other way.

As we drew near our destination, Syringa Provincial Park, we began to see an occasional summer cabin set high up on the banks behind the trees, and then, finally, a boat with two fishermen happily hauling in trout. We knew, then, that we were at the end of the lowest stretch of the Columbia that is true wilderness. From here to the mouth six hundred and fifty miles downstream, the hand of man would be visible on the River. There would always be a highway, a railroad cut, houses, something that would proclaim that man had been here. Quite a difference from the part we had just left, where there were only occasionally signs that this region had ever been changed since first it emerged from the grip of the Ice Age. Still that is part of the mystique of the Columbia, part of the whole, and if I were to examine the whole length of the River, I must perforce take its developed portions along with the beautiful unchanged wilderness we had experienced in its upper reaches. Nevertheless, reaching our destination was something of an anticlimax. Beauty is a commodity for which Bruce and I each have an insatiable appetite, which is probably why we enjoyed this trip so much, for the Arrow Lakes provide it in magnum portions. The sight of a flotilla of white-winged sailboats at the lower end told us that from now on the wild beauty would be tempered by the hand of man, and not all of that would necessarily be ugly or unharmonious.

Hugh Keenleyside Dam, named for a high executive of British Columbia Hydro, Ltd., became operational in 1968 and backs up the River as far as Revelstoke. It stabilizes the seven-and-a-half million acre-feet of water on which we had been so agreeably cruising and has drowned out a few decaying villages left over from the ancient days of steam. Now it helps regulate the flow of water down the main stream of the Columbia and dampen out the floods that formerly were a constant threat downstream.

At Brilliant, near Castlegar, the Kootenay flows into the Columbia, thereby considerably increasing the volume of the River. High on a rocky bluff overlooking the junction surrounded by a high wire fence and flower beds is the massive white concrete tomb of a most unusual man: Peter "the Lordly" Verigin, the uncrowned king of the Doukhobors.

THE DOUKHOBORS, meaning "spirit wrestlers" in Russian, were a sect of the Russian Orthodox Church who migrated to Canada to escape the persecutions they suffered in the Old Country, and especially the compulsory military service imposed by the czar. Regarding all men as brothers, they refused to recognize temporal rulers and many governmental rules. It was bound to get them in trouble, so in 1899 several thousands of them migrated to the boundless lands of the New World, where they hoped to be left alone to live out their own lives their way. After several moves, they finally came to the Nelson-Castlegar area in British Columbia.

Verigin joined them in 1902. A large, handsome man who lived up to his name "The Lordly," he was a born organizer and natural leader who channeled the hard work and agricultural genius of his followers into large holdings at Nelson, Castlegar, and Grand Forks. A consummate diplomat, he somehow got the Canadian government to go along with the Doukhobors' ideas on schooling (unnecessary after the eighth grade, and they ran their own), property ownership (they held their lands in common), and military conscription (they were unalterably opposed to it, even in wartime). In order to conform even in some small degree to British Columbia law, Peter Verigin was the owner of record of all Doukhobor property in British Columbia, making him by far the largest private landowner in the province.

The Doukhobors lived in large, square communal buildings, all built on the same pattern around a huge brick oven from which issued some of the best bread ever baked. There were communal rooms for praying, meeting, and eating; only in sleeping was a family afforded any privacy. Since this was an accepted way of life, and one motivated by a strong religious belief, it generally worked very well, and the colonies flourished mightily. Although the Doukhobors were admirable, hard-working, bill-paying citizens, they had little or no contact with the rest of the Canadians. They remained Russians enclaved in a Canadian land, speaking their own language and intermarrying only within their group. Peter Verigin was their voice, their heart, their brain. He was also their unquestioned master and allegedly arrogated to himself certain personal rights that had perished with other feudal lords during the French Revolution.

Peter had a dozen or so handmaidens, always picked from the prettiest girls in his flock. While this was supposed to be a great honor, there were evidently some sweethearts and brothers who didn't agree, and it has been conjectured that this was one of the causes for the seeds of dissent within the sect. This dissent led to a split within the community. One of these splinter groups, the radical Sons of Freedom, were definitely opposed to public schooling, especially for any Doukhobor children, and backed up their position with strategically placed dynamite explosions. Even within the main group, all of Verigin's dynamism could not control the dissent among some of the younger people who had been born in Canada and considered themselves Canadians first and Doukhobors only second.

On October 28, 1924, Verigin boarded a train with Maria Strevliova, his current handmaiden. He changed his destination enroute, but before he got there, a charge of dynamite placed under his seat blew him, Maria, and the train to bits. The perpetrators were never found, but an educated guess is that someone didn't like Peter or some of his ideas and prerogatives.

With his death, the Doukhobors came upon dark days. His son, Peter the second, tried to stem the tide, but the writing was already on the wall. One by one the communes closed, and their occupants were absorbed into the mainstream of Canadian life. Now, in Castlegar, Nelson, Grand Forks, and other former Doukhobor strongholds, the telephone directories have numerous names of Russian derivation, often belonging to families that regrettably don't speak a word of Russian. But the same industry and thrift that built the Doukhobor empire is still evident in many businesses whose Canadian owners have Russian-sounding names . . . and on the high bluff overlooking the Kootenay, the floodlit tomb of Peter Verigin is still the goal of many a respectful pilgrimage.

Near the airport at Castlegar is a "Doukhobor Village," complete with a square-built, double-storied communal home that is a factual reconstruction of a Doukhobor establishment as it was in the heyday of the community. Complete in every detail, this very well done museum allows the present-day visitor a good insight into what is undoubtedly one of British Columbia's most colorful chapters.

Castlegar is a pleasant town often regarded as a bedroom community for nearby Trail. This is no longer true. Castlegar has a large paper mill and industries of its own, although undoubtedly many of its people do make the thirty-kilometer trek to Trail and its smelters. One of the unique features of the Castlegar–Robson area is a free ferry that operates between the two towns across the Columbia, making the round trip every few minutes.

From Castlegar downriver to Trail, the River runs swiftly between granite hills that look very sparsely wooded in spite of the best efforts made to restore their original forest cover. And thereby hangs a tale.

The industrial colossus of eastern British Columbia is the former Consolidated Mining and Smelting Company of Canada, Ltd., known as Cominco for short. At Trail it operates the world's largest lead and zinc smelter, and no one in this area is immune from its influence, for as Cominco goes, so does Trail and, to a lesser degree, Castlegar, Rossland, and the surrounding towns.

Cominco's site at Trail expresses its dominance of the place. It towers over the city on a plateau overlooking the business district. Its many stacks, some of them belching smoke and steam in spite of the best efforts made to suppress them spread a pall over the city that cannot be completely ignored or explained away. It also provides a standard of living that is the highest in eastern British Columbia and compares favorably with any other city in the province. It is a paradox that the very thing that in past years gave Trail the reputation of being an ugly city is also the same thing that buys its new cars, vacations to Hawaii, and memberships in fancy country clubs.

Like many other towns in British Columbia, Trail was born of a gold strike but grew rich refining copper, lead, zinc, and silver. There are a thousand stories of rich stakes, of barkeeps who grew wealthy by taking stock in payment for their goods in the early days, or wheeler-dealers who would sell one claim to buy another; but our story is of the River, and that story is fascinating enough for throughout the history of Trail, the River has played an important and often dominant part. What is there today is a city of twelve thousand people whose destiny is bound to the market price of zinc, lead, and silver, but who worry far more over the standing of their world-famous hockey team, the Trail Smokeaters.

Trail people don't mind grousing about their town, which especially in the old days before pollution abatement was a synonym for ugliness, but let anyone from the outside say anything against it, and the silence is suddenly pregnant with potential violence. Trail sprawls up and down the steep sides of Trail Creek, now confined in a concrete conduit, and the rocky banks of the Columbia which splits the town in two and connects the halves with bridges. The town, to me, has a vaguely European look, not at all unusual in that Trail has one of the most varied ethnic mixes in the whole province. The houses, built usually on steep hillsides, are small and, even on the lower, flatter stretches where the more affluent people seem to congregate, have very small yards. Space is valuable in Trail, and every inch of it is used. The only outfit that seems to have room to spread is Cominco, and it sprawls all over the plateau from which it dominates the town.

It is only fair to state that Trail, like olives, can become an acquired taste, and once acquired, nothing else is quite like it. There are many beauty spots in the town where Canadians, with their usual love of flowers and gardening, have transfomed rocky ledges into glowing beds of color, and some of the vistas from homes set high up in the rocky hills are absolutely magnificent. The beer is good, and the pastrami the best this side of New York. There is also very good spaghetti to be had in Trail, probably a legacy of its large Italian colony. Cominco is a benevolent employer and has furnished the town with many of the amenities usually found only in larger cities.

The smelters first came to Trail because of the rich copper strikes at nearby Rossland, some ten kilometers away. Ore from the mines was shipped down the river to Northport, across the border in the United States, then shipped back as refined metal. It did not take long for the ore producers to figure out that the substantial shipping costs were eating into their profits, and they built their own smelter, then added to it as further strikes of lead and zinc at the nearby Sullivan mine in Kimberly demanded a more diversified operation. Trail was on the way to becoming the Pittsburgh of the West; but what it gained in profits, it lost in beauty, for the ore roasted here was high in sulphur and killed off the vegetation, hence the nearby naked hills.

World War I gave Trail its first big boost. Lead, zinc, and silver were needed in unprecedented quantities. The ore was available (although the copper that gave Trail its start has long since been depleted) and given a chance, Trail could refine it. The trouble was that although the natives of Trail had long since become accustomed to the mordant brew they laughingly called air, other lesser souls had not, and they objected violently to what the Trail smelters were doing to the atmosphere. Complicating the problem was the fact that air currents know no frontier, and clouds of noxious gas were wafting over the border and putting a definite strain on amicable relations with the United States. Still, everyone needed the metals.

It was really a chemical problem, and the solution was found in chemistry. The stack gas produced by roasting a high-sulphur-content ore contains a high percentage of sulphur dioxide, the villain that had been peeling paint, stunting vegetation, and raising the ire of anyone forced to breath its pungent stench. Sulphur dioxide, when passed through a suitable catalytic agent such as platinum, becomes sulphur trioxide, which, dissolved in water, becomes sulphuric acid, the most indispensable of all industrial chemicals. What had been a liability almost overnight became an asset.

The technological level of any civilization can be accurately gauged by the amount of sulphuric acid it produces, and by this standard the Trail area is technologically advanced indeed, for suddenly it had oceans of the vitriolic stuff. Again, the cost of shipment predicated that it be used locally. And that's how Cominco got into

the fertilizer business. The acid was reacted with phosphate rock and other appropriate raw materials, and Elephant Brand fertilizer became a common name throughout the farming regions of the Northwest. Also, the air became appreciably cleaner.

Air quality has been a long and continuing battle for Cominco — it started thirty years before it was required by law — but now the quality of the air over their town is no worse than that over any other comparable industrial site, and better than most. All emanations from the stacks go first through an elaborate filtering device that passes the effluent through tightly woven fabric bags that filter out several tons of particulate matter every day, much of it valuable metal, and scrubbers that effectively remove gaseous and particulate impurities.

Cominco people realize that in an operation of its size, in which complex chemical reactions are involved, many of them using temperatures so high that metals are actually vaporized, some degradation of the environment is inevitable. Their aim, therefore, is to keep the pollution level as low as technologically possible and then, once that standard has been achieved, raise the standard and start all over again. The efforts cost millions, but the company considers it money well spent. After all, the town is populated by Cominco people and their well-being will have a direct relationship to how well the company grows and prospers. You very seldom hear a complaint on the state of the ecology from Trail people; they recognize all too well the source of their prosperity, and on the few occasions when the air assumes a bit of the tang for which it was once infamous, they sniff it appreciatively. As one of them told me, "That smells like bacon and eggs to me!"

Some of the purest metals in the world come from this Cominco plant, for one division of the company produces highly refined metals of analytical quality. Ore from as far away as the Northwest Territories, a thousand miles north under the shadow of the Arctic Circle, is refined here, using enough natural gas and electrical energy to service a very large city. Cominco owns five large hydroelectric plants on the Kootenay River and one on the Pend Oreille,

Franklin Delano Roosevelt Lake, impounded by the Grand Coulee Dam, reaches to the Canadian Border.

and while the amount of electricity used in the refining process is not public knowledge, it is safe to assume it is considerable. Large rooms filled with electrolytic cells day and night deposit refined, almost totally pure lead and zinc on cathode plates, which are melted down and cast into pure ingots that help feed the metal needs of the world. From the impurities left by the refining process, silver and gold are recovered. Melted into bars worth thousands of dollars each, the bullion is stacked like cordwood by employees who have long since stopped equating what they handle so casually with enormous amounts of money.

Large quantities of water are also used by the Cominco plant, and the sight of six or seven huge pipes returning this water from the plant into the River is very unnerving to one who, only forty miles above this site, was unhesitatingly drinking from the River. I am assured that the effluent dumped into the Columbia is mostly inert slag and subject to very strict Provincial controls, but somehow I get the idea that drinking from the Columbia below Trail would be a rather sporting proposition.

The River below Trail has a few interesting white spots all the way into the United States. Just a hundred yards above the border but still definitely in Canada, the Pend Oreille, which is an American river for the much greater part of its length, boils into the Columbia as the last Canadian tributary of the River.

Below here, the River becomes a naturalized American, but it must always be remembered that the River is Canadian by birth. The importance of the Upper Columbia cannot be overemphasized, and this is the reason why the treaty of 1964 which governs the international development of the Columbia is considered a landmark. The storage areas in Canada are of the utmost importance to the proper maintenance of stream flow, and it is for this reason that the United States agreed to finance the upstream dams, which will of course ultimately redound to the mutual benefit of the two countries. In spite of occasional bickerings, the amicable way the problems confronting these two neighbors in the control of a mutually shared natural resource have been solved provides an example to other countries and shows what can be done when neighbors decide to work together, rather than at cross-purposes. We will talk further about these problems when we discuss dams in a future chapter.

Just below the United States border, the headwaters of Franklin Delano Roosevelt Lake begin. Northport, the first United States town on the Columbia, was once the site of a larger smelter feeding off the ores of Rossland and local limestone. The building of the Trail smelter finished off the local industry, and now there is not much there other than a sawmill.

The banks of the River are sparsely wooded all the way to Grand Coulee, some 120 miles downstream. The lake has been in its bed now for some thirty-five years, but the banks still are not completely stabilized, as huge slides into the water will testify. This is an unusually beautiful part of the reservoir, with several outstanding vistas visible from the highway.

One of the best dividends from the impoundment of the waters of the Columbia by Grand Coulee Dam is the recreational wonderland created along Highway 25 — a wonderland not yet fully discovered or utilized. The highway follows the lake for many miles, and there are hundreds of choice camp spots and beaches, many of them fully developed — and mostly empty. As one who has repeatedly made full use of these superb recreational sites, I am grateful but still somewhat puzzled as to why others have not yet found out that this is one of the most beautiful, unspoiled reaches of clean river still left in the United States.

Kettle Falls, on Highway 25, is a historic spot, although the original site is now drowned by the lake created by Grand Coulee Dam. For many years it was the site of Fort Colville, the largest Hudson's Bay Company post in the interior. This was a natural trading spot, for from time immemorial the Indians had congregated here to harvest the salmon trying desperately to leap the huge falls where the Columbia plunged over a twenty-five foot cliff. The produce of the coastal tribes, mostly dried fish and shell beads, woven bark, and canoes, was traded for furs and buffalo hides, stone arrowheads, and slaves from the interior country. The Colvilles were the traders of the interior largely because of the strategic location of Kettle Falls, which made a land passage mandatory. After the Hudson's Bay post was established, it became an even greater center of commerce, for the white man's goods coming up the river from Fort Vancouver were in great demand by the inland tribes, who quickly realized the advantages of a steel knife over one of chipped stone.

At Kettle Falls the Jesuits maintained St.

Paul's Mission. It was a center of missionary effort among the Indians which attained a high degree of success. Catholic missionaries, who from their long association with voyageurs and almost two hundred and fifty years of missionary efforts among the Indians had a much better understanding of Indian mentality than did their stiffer Protestant counterparts, usually enjoyed very good success among the tribes of the Northwest. By 1844 they counted four dioceses, eleven chapels, three schools, a college for boys, twenty-six clergymen, seven nuns, and over six thousand converts. Considering the temper of the times, it is no wonder that their success was a constant source of strife and envy on the part of their equally hard-working, but much less successful Protestant contemporaries. The original St. Paul's Mission sits in a grove of pine trees, two hundred yards from the road to the bridge crossing the Columbia, preserved as a national historic site.

South of Kettle Falls the River, still affording gorgeous vistas, beautiful camp sites, and unused beaches is bordered by Highway 25 as far as Miles, where the Spokane joins the River. The rest of the Columbia to Grand Coulee is roadless, although the boater will find unusually beautiful water and exceptional camp sites, some of them fully developed with fireplaces, tables, and privies. This is fine for those who enjoy these amenities, and many do. Personally, I like to pitch my camp on some deserted beach, build a small cooking fire in a ring of stones I have built myself, eat my meal out of a messkit, then sleep under the stars. And this section of the river, bordered on the north side by the Colville Indian Reservation, offers just that kind of camping. This, in my estimation, is one of the most beautiful, least known, and most unused sections of the Northwest. A trip from Miles to Coulee Dam on a warm summer day counted less than a dozen people and scores of uncluttered beaches along absolutely idyllic stretches of river. For some unknown reason, this part of the River hasn't caught on as a recreational area, probably because a paved road doesn't lead directly to it. Personally, I hope it never does; this section of the River is much too beautiful to be littered with beer cans.

The Colville Indian Reservation was the site of the banishment of the "Red Napoleon," Chief Joseph of the Nez Percé, after his hopeless war with the United States Cavalry in 1877. Given the beauty of this area, one might wonder why anyone would object to ending his days in such a beautiful place. The answer, of course, is that it was not his native home and, beautiful as this land is, it still pales in comparison to the valley in the shadow of the Wallowa peaks, one of the most spectacularly beautiful valleys in the Columbia River watershed. Chief Joseph lies buried at Nespelem, which is the tribal headquarters for the Colville Indian Confederation. Visiting his grave was for me the fulfillment of a childhood dream, for as a boy back in my native Vermont, he was one of my childhood heroes, and I had always hoped to someday visit his grave, to pay my personal respects to this, one of the greatest Americans who ever lived.

The vegetation along the banks has now begun to change from a wooded to a desert ecology. The stands of trees grow thinner and farther apart, while occasional clumps of sagebrush and other desert vegetation make their first appearance. The River is about to undergo its first major metamorphosis, from a mountain river, flowing through mountainous country, to a desert river with a completely different character. It is one of the changes that makes the Columbia many rivers, each one different, each one fascinating. And the dividing line is just around the next bend.

The Middle River

WITH THE POSSIBLE EXCEPTION of the Great Wall of China or the Panama Canal, few structures on Earth have had such an effect on the course of human events as has Grand Coulee Dam, the concrete monolith that divides the upper and middle portions of the Columbia River. Its story will be told in a separate chapter, but now we are more concerned with it as a landmark on our journey to the sea. Below the dam, the River assumes a very different character. It ceases to be a wild, scenic river and becomes instead a working river—one still endowed with its own particular beauty, but somehow transmuted from a mountain into a desert river.

Before Grand Coulee was built, there was very little reason for anyone to visit the area where the dam now stands. It was a sparsely populated desert, with the River flowing between increasingly high canyon walls, a region that offered no incentive for a visit unless one were interested in desert ecology or gaunt, sunbaked scenery. Now, Grand Coulee Dam is one of the prime tourist attractions of the United States, and the desert country that has blossomed as the result of its presence is every year

The rich rolling hills near Walla Walla raise some of the world's finest white soft wheat.

invaded by thousands of appreciative visitors who go back home extolling its beauty and so perpetuate the flow.

An appreciation of the desert as a place of beauty is an acquired taste, and one which not all people achieve, even after long exposure to it. It is paradoxical in that a full appreciation and understanding of a desert's beauty entails achieving seemingly antithetical ends. A desert is a vastness, space, an expanse of barren country with no distraction to hinder the spirit from soaring to limitless heights. And yet, the desert is also a region of teeming life, a microcosm of specialized adaptation amazing in its complexity. To really know and understand a desert, you must not only look at its limitless horizon, but also get down on your knees to examine the ground at your feet, and only in the full appreciation of both views can your knowledge be complete.

For the next five hundred miles, the River flows through this kind of country.

The Columbia has two "Big Bends," the first one on the Upper River, where the river flanks the Selkirks, and the second one after the river leaves Grand Coulee and heads north, then westward. The sixty-mile-long lake impounded behind Chief Joseph Dam flows through desert country—a country of high, mostly barren plateaus and naked rock. A desolate land, and yet one that exerts a strange, almost mystical fascination. It is easy to understand, in this type of country, why the world's great religions were born in primarily desert lands: there is something about great spaces and loneliness that engenders in a man a sense of the proper relation between himself and the cosmic forces that led to his creation. Rufus Woods, the dynamic publisher of the *Wenatchee World,* whose editorials were one of the chief motivating forces that led to the building of Grand Coulee Dam, well understood this country. It is only fitting that the lake impounded behind Chief Joseph Dam was named in his honor.

While the main river from the base of Grand Coulee Dam turns northward, there is also part of the Columbia that turns southward, and this branch has an importance out of all proportion to its size. Pumped up from Roosevelt Lake by six of the world's largest pumps, 1,600 cubic feet of irrigation water flow into the Feeder Canal every second and from there into Banks Lake, which is simply part of the Grand Coulee, the former bed of the Columbia River,

with a dam at the lower end. From there, irrigation waters flow by gravity to the Columbia Basin Project.

Banks Lake, with its perpendicular basalt walls from which colorful waterfalls drop into the lake during spring runoff, is a rapidly expanding recreational area in which more and more people take advantage of the unique blend of desert scenery and cool, clean water it affords. Boating and fishing are excellent, and well-developed campgrounds are proliferating to take care of the expanding demand.

A few miles below the dam, on the rim of a cirquelike canyon, there is a roadside museum with an excellent display of what caused the natural wonder visible from the museum window: Dry Falls, one of the greatest natural wonders of the Northwest. A semicircular cliff about four hundred feet in height and several miles long was once the site of the greatest cataract on the North American continent. The Columbia, then a giant at least forty times as large as it is today, once poured over these cliffs the waters from nearby glaciers when those ice sheets were advancing. An ice dam, somewhere upriver but most probably just about where Grand Coulee Dam stands today, diverted the river from its ancient bed and tore out a new one where the River presently flows. The ancient bed is now the Grand Coulee, with Banks Lake neatly ensconced in its depths, and Dry Falls, with a few small scattered lakes at its feet: a pale reminder of what must have been one of the most stupendous sights this planet has ever provided.

To really appreciate Dry Falls, one should take the circuitous road from the Sun Lakes Park and drive or walk to the small lakes below the museum. There the size of the cliffs can be appreciated, but even a vivid imagination can only begin to picture what a sight this roaring, thundering mass of cascading water must have been, way back at the ending of the Ice Age.

The fantastic force of the surging waters rolled boulders as big as trucks along the riverbed, gouging it out ever deeper, until they became smooth and polished: the giant megaliths that can still be observed along the ancient bed of the river and along its banks. It would take forces as titanic as these to rip open mountains of solid basalt, and usually these forces would have to be applied for thousands of years before the tough crust of the earth would yield enough to allow the imprisoned waters to finally find their way to their parent sea. Actually, some of the most spectacular canyons along this stretch of the River were torn out at the height of the Great Spokane Flood, which mustered volumes of water and vectoral forces so immense that the work of centuries was achieved in a matter of weeks.

Those raging waters have left a legacy of desert lakes, where whirling currents once rolled giant boulders in circular paths and wore out huge holes that today constitute the Sun Lakes. Glacial ice helped, shaping the lakes into elongated fingers, often many hundreds of feet deep, so that today's recreationist can find, on a desert land whose fringes are agreeably warmed by a desert sun, deep pockets of ice cold water. And finally, man came and, by raising the water table all through this region with his irrigation efforts, added to the expanse of the lakes and made them into the summer playgrounds they are today.

There is no question about the popularity of the Sun Lakes. Tree fringed, clean and clear, a veritable oasis in the desert, they are some of the most frequented playgrounds in Washington State even though when they were first suggested as a site for a state park, some legislators thought the idea was an elaborate practical joke.

Not all the lakes on the scenic route to Othello are developed. Blue Lake and Lake Lenore have been left largely in their primitive state and get plenty of use from people who prefer their surroundings to be unstructured by man. This route is one of the most unexpectedly scenic roads in all Washington. I say unexpectedly because who would expect to find a water-dominated scenic route in the middle of the dessert? A related phenomenon is the famed Summer Falls near Ephrata, where the water from a canal thunders over a forty-foot cliff in a rainbow of drenching spray–during the summer months only, for this is irrigation water.

Bridgeport, once a roaring steamboat town, is now more famous as the site of Chief Joseph Dam, the first dam below Grand Coulee, and for the fine fruit grown in the region. Brewster, a few miles downstream where the Okanogan comes into the Columbia, is likewise a fruit-packing center, but also well known as the site of COMSAT, a communications station where a huge 108-foot parabolic reflector both beams messages to and receives them from an orbiting communications satellite 24,500 miles out in space. Brewsterites are proud of this but would

rather talk about their basketball team and coach, both of whom are highly regarded not only locally but throughout the state. Pateros, where the Methow River joins the Columbia, got its name during the Spanish-American War from a town in the Philippines where some of the local boys saw action. Just south of the apple orchards of Pateros, the banks of the Columbia are littered with nomads, huge rounded boulders brought down by the glaciers and left standing there when the ice receded.

The waters of the Columbia here are backed up by Wells Dam, one of the most unusual dams on the River, and the last one to provide passage for anadromous fish. Built by the Douglas County Public Utilities District in 1967, this is the first in line of four dams on the main stem of the Columbia built and operated by public utility districts. The display rooms at the dam, open to the public, have an excellent showing of the salmon's life cycle and the part the dam plays in it.

All the way from Bridgeport past Wenatchee, the Columbia Valley is one huge fruit orchard. The combination of stony soil rich in minerals, plentiful sun, and good drainage apparently is just the right combination for growing superior fruit, while the chilly late summer nights attendant to a desert environment add a touch of color that supplies the visual appeal so necessary for today's marketing success.

While it is my intention to follow as closely as possible the mainstem of the Columbia, there are a few detours that should be made if I am to bring some far-off reader the true feeling of the Columbia River country, and one of these detours is at Chelan Falls. The river comes busily tumbling down a rocky gorge only four miles after it emerges from a mountain lake deservedly famous as one of the great aesthetic experiences of this world. Lake Chelan should not be compared to any other body of water, for while it may have many of the characteristics of Lake Como, or Baikal, or a Norwegian fjord, to all of which it has been compared, it is uniquely itself. Chelan is Chelan, and is beyond comparison. Lake Slocan, another glacial lake in British Columbia, comes the closest, but even here the comparison pales.

The native Indians were the first people to fall under the spell of its beauty, for the name Chelan means "beautiful water." The first writers who saw it may be forgiven if their prose approached rhapsodic poetry in describing it, for few bodies of water anywhere on the face of this planet so richly merit all the praise and wonderstruck awe that generations of viewers have accorded it. A silver-blue streak of glacial water winding into the heart of the Cascades, it reflects neat rows of orchards at its foot, glacier-topped mountains drained by a roaring white-water river at its head, and in between seventy miles of sandy beaches, steep cliffs, crystal clear water, foaming cataracts, and one incredible vista after another, each one seemingly more spectacular than the last.

The lifeline of the lake is a diesel-powered fifty-foot boat, the *Lady of the Lake,* which in summertime daily makes the round trip to Stehekin, a hamlet near the head of the lake, carrying freight and a capacity load of enthralled passengers. For the first twenty-five miles, the lake is bordered by orchard covered hills with

Sheer basaltic walls flank Banks Lake.

occasional sandy beaches relieving the steep slopes that plunge into the blue depths. Roads run along either shore and cottages cling precariously to increasingly steep hills. At Twenty-Five Mile Creek the road ends, and further travel up the lake is strictly by boat. The granite cliffs are at first sparsely covered by trees springing tenaciously from rocky fissures and then gradually become more heavily wooded as the lake penetrates the Cascades into areas of greater rainfall.

The *Lady* pauses at several designated stops along the lake, delivering mail, groceries, motorbikes, live poultry, or even pulling in to some rocky point in answer to the vigorously waved towel of a hiker who has belatedly discovered that the almost perpendicular shores of the lake are not conducive to hiking. And when it finally pulls in at Stehekin, where its arrival is the social highlight of the day, it disgorges its passengers into a mountain valley that leads into the very heart of the North Cascades and to some of the most beautiful, spectacular mountain scenery in the United States. From the ter-

race of the small, busy restaurant, one can look across the lake to a mountain rising almost perpendicularly from the depths while the water changes its colors by the minute as the sun throws an ever-changing pattern of light and shadow across the opposite shore. This constant change of light and color is one of Lake Chelan's greatest charms, and the big reason why a large percentage of the *Lady of the Lake's* passengers are people who have been there before. No two trips are alike: ask five people who have been to the head of the lake to describe Mount Jackson and its satellite peaks and you'll get five different descriptions, unless they all happened to have been there at the same time.

Lake Chelan is the epitome of what a mountain lake should be: crystal clear, mountain bordered, teeming with fish, remote, yet accessible and forever changing, so that no one ever completely knows all its faces; and therein may be the secret of its charm. Lake Chelan is a stormy, capricious beauty who welcomes your advances yet always remains unconquered. It is entirely fitting that the water from this gem of the Cascades should find its way to the sea by way of the Columbia, which although surfeit with beauty can always make room for one more jewel in its crown of glory.

The river below Chelan Falls flows gently, for its waters are backed up into a lake by Rocky Reach Dam. Entiat, with its busy fruit warehouses, sits on the right bank, basking in the prosperity brought to it by the scarlet and gold bounty of its orchards. Earthquake Point is also in this stretch of the River, a spot of considerable interest to history and geology buffs, for here at the turn of the century an earthquake split off a massive section of the cliff bordering the Columbia and effectively dammed it for almost twenty-four hours. The river downstream ran dry, much to the consternation of the superstitious Indians, who were convinced that the gods of the Columbia had been angered and so had stopped the flow of the River. Before the elaborate plans to placate the gods could be implemented, the River breached the landslide and its normal flow was resumed. Today, only a fractured cliff—a geological bonanza—and a new bend in the River commemorate the event.

Rocky Reach Dam, some five miles above Wenatchee, is especially noteworthy for the excellent exhibits it stages. If ever you've wondered how the power of falling water somehow becomes the energy that warms your morning coffee, here's the chance to find out. The display about the story of electricity is extremely well done, as are the displays on the geological and ethnological histories on Rocky Reach. The fish ladders—a series of small waterfalls which the salmon can leap with ease—with their provocative message, "Look a Salmon in the Eye," are also very popular and very well patronized.

Just as Lake Chelan is a masterpiece of natural beauty, so Wenatchee can also boast of a

Ohme Gardens, near Wenatchee, show what labor, loving care, and water can do to a barren desert plateau.

unique attraction, this one man-made but also undeniably the work of a master. High on a cliff to the right, just before reaching the city limits, there is a cluster of green trees and luxuriant, colorful vegetation. Green trees? On a clifftop surrounded by nothing but the scrubbiest sagebrush?

Puzzlement is as good a frame of mind as any in which to approach Ohme Gardens, since before you complete your visit, you'll be more puzzled than ever. How could a barren, rocky hilltop possibly be transformed into a fairyland of massed flower banks, cool dark groves, and mirroring pools? Yet the miracle is undoubtedly real, and it is here for your entertainment as well as amazement.

The answer, of course, lies in the application of liberal quantities of water, imagination bordering on genius, and hard work spanning two generations. The result is a fairyland of colorful vegetation, meticulously clipped lawns, and artfully contrived vistas that are as beautiful as they are improbable. Ohme Gardens does relatively little promotion, other than local signs indicating its entrance, yet such is its word-of-mouth advertising that every year the flow of visitors increases almost geometrically. On weekends and holidays the seven-acre site is crowded with happy people who just can't understand how this miracle came to be but are supremely pleased that someone, somehow, turned the trick.

It all started back in the twenties when the present owner's father bought a section of orchard land and in the process acquired this steep, rocky promontory as part of the bargain, thrown in almost as an afterthought, because it evidently had no value. Much too steep and rocky for orchard use, it was considered worthless land. Mr. Ohme, however, began playing with it as a hobby, a respite from the unremitting toil of the orchardist. Of German-Swiss descent, he decided to see if he could recreate in a small way the Alpine scenery he so much admired. He started small: only a few trees shading a hole that he had painfully excavated in the solid rock and piped for water. The trees, natives of the nearby Cascades, flourished with the abundant moisture and attention showered on them. Encouraged, he expanded his efforts and laid flagstones fronting a rustic open shed where the family for many years had its gatherings. Using only plants native to the region, he little by little expanded the irrigated spot until

it covered almost an acre. By this time, the original trees were quite large and the transplanted flowers were spreading anywhere the water was available. In thirty years of loving labor, the fledgling project grew to three acres and became increasingly lovely as plants took root and perpetuated themselves. Soon the hobby was taking up most of Ohme's time and retirement years, and by the time it passed into the hands of his son, Gordon Ohme, it already was a full-time job.

It also was a noted beauty spot, for the family, after much urging, had begun to share its treasure with other members of the community. Expanded every year so that it now covers almost seven acres, it is a living, growing thing that changes its face almost weekly and is always entrancing. Scores of chipmunks and cottontail rabbits have found it to be a haven and have become so tame they will take tidbits right out of the visitor's hand.

Probably the best tribute to the beauty of Ohme Gardens is the complete absence of litter—and that, in itself, says quite a bit. The paths, most of them clambering up and down the steep side of the hills, are made of carefully fitted flagstones and lead to rustic seats set at strategic viewpoints. In spite of the steepness of the paths, people of all ages negotiate them, probably drawing strength from the beauty that surrounds them.

One of the most beautiful vistas from the Garden entrance is that of the city of Wenatchee framed in trees. I freely admit that Wenatchee is one of my favorite towns, but even the unbiased would find much to admire in this busy, pretty little city. The streets are broad, clean, and well laid out. The residential area boasts of many fine, well-kept homes, the people are friendly and helpful, and besides the many fine hotel accommodations, one can easily obtain a civilized meal in Wenatchee, something not always available in much larger places. The center of fruit production in the Columbia River Valley, it is largely oriented to that industry and each spring plays host to thousands of appreciative visitors who help it celebrate its Apple Blossom Festival with town-wide festivities, complete with elaborate floats and some very pretty girls. In the winter, the town is full of skiers, for the runs of Mission Ridge, only twelve miles out of town, offer something for everyone, whether rankest snow-bunny or hot-shot expert.

Wenatchee is built on a broad, sloping shelf of the Columbia River and has been a fruit-growing center from its earliest days. It also was a center of steamboat activity, which will be treated in a later chapter, and those robust days definitely left its mark on the town's character. The orchards really multiplied after 1904, when a canal brought irrigation waters from the Wenatchee River to the uplands. Suddenly, these stony lands began producing fruit at a prodigious rate, so that today Wenatchee produces a volume of apples, peaches, cherries, plums, and pears out of all proportion to its size. The orchards start right at the edge of town and inch higher and higher up the surrounding hills every year as more land, through the miracle of irrigation, is brought into cultivation.

The largest single employer in the Wenatchee area is the Aluminum Corporation of America, Alcoa for short, which has a large plant ten miles out of town at Rock Island. Built during the Korean War to supply aluminum for aircraft, it has a payroll of over one thousand people and has a significant impact on the economy of the region. The plant is located there simply because of the availability of large quantities of hydroelectric energy at favorable rates, something that is imperative in a process which by its very nature consumes vast quantities of electrical energy. From Alcoa's five potlines and casting machine, a constant supply of aluminum ingots issues, to be fashioned elsewhere into the many products for which this space-age metal is so well suited.

Rock Island was the first dam on the main-stem Columbia to generate electrical energy. Situated right next to the highway, it puts on quite a show during periods of high water, for it spills an impressive tonnage in full view of the tourists, most of whom had no idea of the volume of water carried by this stream. New powerhouse facilities on the right bank house eight generators, each weighing over eleven hundred tons. It is interesting to note that the rotors and stators of these monstrous machines, each unit weighing an impressive 900,000 pounds, were shipped up the Columbia by barge as far as Priest Rapids. There, a powerful crawler-type transporter carried them around the dam to another barge which floated the load to Wanapum Dam. There, it was again transported around the dam to complete its journey, again by barge, to Rock Island. It was the single heaviest load ever transported this far up the Columbia by

water, and it dramatically illustrated the strategic role the Columbia plays in the transportation of the Pacific Northwest.

Below Rock Island, the road turns sharply away from the river, which it will not reach again until Vantage. The River takes a sharp bend to the right and proceeds down a steep-walled canyon for almost twenty-five roadless miles, first passing a resort area in the shadow of towering seven-hundred-foot cliffs at Crescent Bar. The canyon is a very interesting and picturesque stretch of river, opening up once in a while to beaches with high, rounded sand dunes complete with nude sunbathers, and at other times fenced in by varicolored basalt cliffs from which aquifers pour water into the river. Mostly, these aquifers are fed by seep water from the Columbia Basin Project.

One of the sights that boaters on the river always take in is a huge perpendicular petrified log four hundred feet up on the face of a sheer cliff. Examination with high-powered binoculars will reveal this log to be pockmarked with bullet holes, usually put there by skeptical boaters who do not believe that this seemingly ordinary log is really solid stone. Their wonder is justified, for although petrified trees are common in this area, this one is so spectacularly placed as to invariably excite speculation as to just how it got up there. The ancient voyageurs report this tree in their journals and were probably the first to bounce a bullet off it.

The country between Vantage and Vernita Bridge is desert country at its best—or worst, depending on whether or not you are a desert buff. Flat, either stony or drifting sand, it is oven hot in summer and a windy desolation in winter: seemingly the last place anyone would like to live. Yet, at Desert Aires, a few miles downstream from Wanapum Dam, a colony of homes is already firmly established and growing. It seems that life in the desert can be loads of fun, especially if your home is well insulated and air conditioned and you enjoy the many sports which dwelling in the desert makes possible. This area is also the ancestral home of the Wanapums, a peaceful, fish-oriented Indian tribe that made the mistake of never taking part in a war against the United States. For this reason, they have no treaty rights and no reservation. Consequently, they have pretty well died out as a tribal entity, being reduced by 1981 to three members only, who, fittingly enough, were employed at Wanapum Dam.

The stream below Priest Rapids Dam is also significant in that for almost seventy miles it is the last free-flowing stretch of the Columbia above tidewater left in the United States. The gravelly bed of the river is well adapted to salmon spawning, especially for the royal chinook salmon which spawn on the mainstream of the river and which in the fall spawn here in great numbers. This stretch of the river has been the object of a continuing tug of war between environmentalists intent on keeping the river in its pristine state, and power advocates who visualize one more dam to help alleviate the burgeoning power requirements of the next few decades. With the availability of nuclear energy, the environmentalists' point of view seems to be prevailing, which probably evokes mixed reactions from them, because in order to preserve the river in its present state, they must perforce accede to the building of one more nuclear plant.

Now that the river level is stabilized by dams, riverfront properties near Wenatchee are choice building sites.

When that plant is built, it probably will be on this stretch of the river, for this is the site of the Hanford Atomic Reserve, where nuclear energy is a way of life. The site of the World War II Manhattan Project, it already has one operating nuclear power plant and several others building. Their story will be told more fully in a later chapter, but for the time being it is enough to say that this 636-square-mile preserve is the main center of nuclear energy and research in the United States and, most likely, in the world. The towns that have grown up adjacent to it— Richland and, to a lesser degree, Kennewick and Pasco—are very much influenced by what goes on here.

The river here runs under a line of high white cliffs, past the site of the old fruit-growing town of Hanford, and in the neighorhood of Richland meets the headwaters of the McNary Dam impoundment. Also, at Richland, the Columbia receives the waters of the Yakima River, which drains one of the richest and most interesting parts of the Columbia River country.

THE YAKIMA VALLEY, known today as one the of most fertile and fruitful sections of the United States, would be largely a desert were it not for irrigation water. The Yakima River and its tributaries which rise in the usually snow-rich Cascades are the magic wand whose waters, channeled through canals, siphons, irrigation ditches, and overhead sprinklers, bring the arid soil to rich production and make possible the thriving cities of the Yakima Valley.

The largest of these towns is Yakima, a busy, bustling sun-drenched city that grew rich on the fruit its orchards produce so bountifully and gets still richer every day on the variety of crops modern agricultural methods make possible. In the Moxee area, many thousands of acres of fertile valley land are engaged in growing hops, used in beer; and in the lower valley of the Yakima, grapes are an important crop. Scoffers who had maintained that the Yakima Valley might very well grow grapes suited for grape juice but not for wine were dumbfounded when in the early 1970s, a number of white wines were produced which not only held their own in competition with California's best, but even on several occasions topped the list. Today, new vineyards planted with the vinifera type grapes used in winemaking are springing up all over the valley as growers rush to cash in on the valley's ability to produce wine grapes that are much better than anyone other than a few dreamers had ever imagined.

The lower Yakima Valley has several smaller cities: Sunnyside, Grandview, Granger, and Prosser, all agriculturally oriented and delightful places in which to live. This section of the state is growing quite rapidly, as the word gets around that the quality of life in these small towns is very nearly ideal. Not a few of the new people moving in are refugees from the cities who find in the friendly, slower-paced Yakima Valley a welcome relief from the frenetic pressures of their former lives. The Valley absorbs them all and in a very short time makes them practically indistinguishable from the original inhabitants.

By the time the Yakima reaches the Columbia at Richland, its volume has been so depleted by the needs of the irrigationists that it has a lesser volume at its mouth than it does a hundred miles upstream. And yet, the results of that withdrawal show in a hundred verdant miles growing diversified crops and maintaining a prosperous population of over a hundred thousand people.

The Yakima Valley is indeed a rapidly growing area, but its growth is nothing compared to the Tri-Cities, by actual statistics the fastest growing portion of Washington State. Richland itself is a very young city, for it is the result of the almost overnight construction of the Manhattan Project, which gave the United States the atomic bomb and ended World War II. Much of the activity spilled over into Kennewick and Pasco, which grew from towns of four or five thousand each to four times that many in one generation.

Today, Richland, Pasco, and Kennewick are facing up to the realization that while they are three separate urban entities, they are bound by proximity to a common destiny. The Tri-Cities are already a major metropolitan center, which has a growth potential unexceeded by any other urban area in the Northwest. Each town is different and contributes something of its own flavor to the metropolitan whole, but it is the union of the three, as the Tri-Cities, that captures the imagination, for in this case the whole is indubitably greater than the sum of its parts.

Richland started out as a completely planned company town. Built during the 1943 and 1944 war years, it still shows vestiges of the military barracks style of architecture that was dominant until the town was freed from government control and allowed to develop a personality of its own. Now, some beautiful new homes are being built, as befits a town with a cultured and affluent population, for Richland certainly has one of the highest educational and income levels of any town in the United States. The second generation, children born here during or soon after the war, are raising families of their own, and the town is finally putting down roots. Trees planted during during the construction era to relieve the drab monotony of a desert landscape have now grown to a respectable size, and only an occasional sagebrush-covered sand dune on a vacant lot reminds the visitor that Richland is an oasis. In spite of a somewhat unfinished look, it is a very attractive town with excellent tourist facilities and is becoming a very popular convention center, largely because of the large concentration of intelligent, enthusiastic boosters.

Kennewick has long been considered a bedroom community for its two more dynamic neighbors but definitely has a personality of its own which is preferred by many. More sedate and settled, it boasts wide streets shaded by old trees and a unique pedestrian-oriented downtown shopping mall that has often been copied by other towns. The growth in Kennewick has been mostly in dwellings rather than in industry, and that probably accounts for the quiet beauty of its well-established residential sections. Like all portions of the Tri-Cities, Kennewick lately has experienced an almost explosive growth, and the outskirts of the town see whole new streets constructed and occupied in a matter of months. Much of this growth is on a plain west of the city, in an area that only a few years ago was the exclusive domain of jackrabbits and coyotes.

Pasco, the smallest of the three towns, is probably the liveliest. It grew up as a railroad center, but now barge lines' terminals and a busy modern airport are a significant part of its transportation picture. Situated on the lower end of the Columbia Basin Project, Pasco gets a lot of trade from the new agricultural enterprises springing up all through the area, and it justly feels that its growth has just begun.

Pasco reportedly got its name from a town in Peru which some railway engineer thought was the worst spot he had ever seen. The original site of Pasco reminded him of that site, so, admittedly with some justification, he bestowed the name on the new railroad town. . . . and it stuck. There are those who will tell you that some sections of Pasco still richly deserve the unsavory reputation the whole town formerly held, but these people haven't seen the newer sections of the town, where the landscaping comes in with the water mains. These newer sections represent the best in desert living, with tree-shaded, flower-bordered streets that are establishing new standards of what a well-laid-out town should be.

A few miles downstream from Pasco, the Snake River joins the Columbia, almost doubling the flow of the parent stream. A boisterous, brawling river rich in history, it was the path that Lewis and Clark took; and here at Burbank, they got their first view of the Great River of the West which was to carry them to the sea. Here also was founded the town of Ainsworth, which grew up as the railroad bridge over the Snake was begun in 1879. Ainsworth's span of life was only five years—it died in 1884—but in its heyday it established a record for violence matched only by Walla Walla on a Saturday night.

It was an era of tough towns, but even among the toughest, Ainsworth was something special. Any fight that didn't end in a fatality just wasn't worth mentioning; and fights were a daily event. Even the toughest tracklayer breathed a sigh of relief when the completion of railroad construction brought on Ainsworth's unlamented demise, because simply as a result of the laws of averages, it would have been only a matter of time till he himself became one more footnote in Ainsworth's history of violence.

Another town, downriver, also partook of Ainsworth's colorful notoriety. Near the mouth of the Walla Walla River, there is still a town called Wallula, a quiet little settlement on a sandy rise overlooking Wallula Gap and the original site of the Hudson's Bay post of Fort Walla Walla. This post was an important link in the chain of forts joining Fort Vancouver to the interior and played a large part in the opening of the Oregon Country. Marcus Whitman drew his supplies from Fort Walla Walla, and its name crops up constantly in the narratives of the early pioneers, for with its strategic position at the mouth of the Walla Walla River, it was destined to continue as a town even after the post was abandoned during the Indian Wars in 1856.

The discovery of gold in the Orofino Country in Idaho in 1860 and the advent of the steamboating era on the Columbia gave birth to the town of Wallula, one of the most colorful spots on the entire Columbia. An early chronicler asserts, apparently with some pride, that "its waterfront was the busiest, its saloons the most raucous, its whores the ugliest and its fleas the friendliest of any riverfront town in the Northwest."

Old Wallula is just a memory now, covered by the backwaters of McNary Dam. Most likely, very few of the happy water skiers who glide over its site ever give a thought to the events that took place here and helped make possible the full lives they enjoy today. But shape them they did, for Wallula was the key to the Walla Walla country and, as the terminus of the old Baker Railroad from Walla Walla, played a key role in the development of the interior country and the whole adjacent region.

The Walla Walla River, which joins the Columbia just south of Wallula, contributes a little water and considerable topsoil to the main stream. The area it drains is certainly one of the most interesting in the whole Columbia River system and is steeped in history: in this beautiful, fertile valley ringed by rolling hills and the hazy Blue Mountains, Marcus Whitman established his mission, the Cayuse Wars started, the Great Treaty of 1855 was initiated, and the seeds that were to grow into a Northwest way of life found fertile ground.

Blessed with a mild climate, abundant water, and soil of amazing fertility, Walla Walla was predestined to become a leading agricultural area, but like so many other western towns, its real start came with the magic word *gold*. As early as 1857 a settlement consisting of a stockade and a few crude log cabins had sprung up on Mill Creek near the present site of downtown Walla Walla. Named Steptoeville after the commandant of the cavalry detachment stationed there, it was renamed Walla Walla in 1859, probably to escape the embarrassment engendered by Steptoe's resounding defeat by the Indians near Rosalia. Its big boost came after Asa Pierce, prospecting on the Clearwater near present-day Orofino in 1860, found shiny specks in his placer pan and triggered a gold rush that was to last for a decade.

To a nation still intoxicated with the gold fever of the 1849 California strike, any discovery of the magic metal was bound to engender a stampede. This one was no different. By wagon train, on horseback, singly or in small groups, prospective miners poured into the gold fields. Walla Walla was the only established settlement in the area, although others soon followed, and it got the lion's share of the action. As the last place where a miner could taste "civilization" before he headed into the wilderness, and the first place where he could "blow his poke" when he came out, hopefully loaded with gold dust, Walla Walla overnight blossomed into a roaring, booming frontier town with more than the usual complement of saloons, questionable business establishments. . . . and churches.

Walla Walla today could be regarded as a rich, prim, proper old maid who had quite a time in her youth and is now busily trying to forget it, hiding behind a facade of respectability and established wealth. Many an old, highly respected family can trace its considerable wealth to those roaring days and nights when gunfights on Main Street were routine, the saloons stayed open round the clock, and Walla Walla's reputation as a wide open town was second to none. The oldest bank in the state, the Baker Boyer National Bank, chartered in 1869, still displays in its handsome lobby a pair of gold scales, complete with several ounces of authentic gold dust and small nuggets, relics of the Orofino diggings.

Gold built Walla Walla, but the real wealth of the area was in the deep fertile soil that to this day establishes the solid basis for its sturdy economic health. It is sometimes difficult to imagine, seeing Walla Walla today, that this city of wide, tree-shaded streets, handsome, well-cared-for homes, and a plethora of flowers had such a colorful beginning. Walla Walla is unquestionably one of the more attractive towns in the Northwest, with spacious parks, three colleges in the area, and social and cultural advantages ordinarily available only in cities many times its size. Dry-land wheat farming had already established a solid agricultural base for the area's prosperity, but when in the 1930s, peas were introduced as a second crop on land ordinarily allowed to lie fallow, thereby allowing two cash crops each year, the bonanza began to roll in. Today, Walla Walla is considered the wealthiest town per capita in Washington State, easily living up to the reputation it has had since 1910 of having "more grand pianos, more expensive motor cars, the most vested wealth, and the prettiest girls in the state."

Just below the mouth of the Walla Walla River, the Columbia flows through an awesome gap where the river, thousands of years ago, broke through the Horse Heaven Hills at the time of the Great Spokane Flood. Flowing past the twin monoliths noted by Lewis and Clark (the Twin Sisters), the river is edged for twelve miles by beetling cliffs until they give place to the rolling hills near Umatilla. For the next fifty miles the River flows through a desert landscape that is increasingly being turned into verdant fields through the miracle of modern irrigation.

Nowhere in the West is the old pioneer tradition of making things happen through a combination of hard work, seized opportunity, and a considerable amount of luck exemplified than in the adjacent towns of Hermiston, Umatilla, and Boardman, where an explosive burst of activity is creating an urban complex on lands that only a decade ago were worthless, sun-blasted desert.

Of these three towns, Umatilla is the oldest. Its history stretches back to the heyday of the steamboats, for it was situated on Umatilla Rapids on the Columbia and was a well-established river town in the 1800s. During the railroad-building period, it became a bustling railroad town and then, during the time when McNary Dam was being constructed, a wide open, booming construction town. Each time its chauvinistic citizens predicted that Umatilla was destined for greatness . . . and each time, after a period of promising growth, it settled back to being a sleepy little Western hamlet in which the seeds of greatness somehow never seemed to germinate.

This time the growth has been slower, steadier, but infinitely more promising, for its progress today is rooted in the broad acres brought into fruitful production by the miracle of water pumped from the Columbia by power generated, at least in part, by McNary Dam, the concrete giant that straddles the river a mile or so upstream from the town. The housing units vacated by the dam workers have been filled again by people employed by the industries that have sprung up to supply the needs of the newly burgeoning region, and Umatilla is finally beginning to realize its dreams. The waterfront, a busy grain and timber shipping spot, is bustling,

the business district is full of new buildings and freshly painted signs, and the population figures at the city limits are changed every few months, and always upward.

Hermiston is only six miles from Umatilla, but if its breakneck growth goes on unchecked for only a very few years, the two towns soon will be contiguous. A pretty town adjacent to the Umatilla River, it was for many years a sleepy little place populated by people infinitely happy to have it that way. The establishment of a large ordinance depot nearby during World War II added a permanent payroll to the region and many of the people who came to work there stayed after their working years were done. Hermiston was the quintessential small Western town, although prettier than most. Still, it was a backwater, off the mainstream of progress, and seemingly destined to stay that way or follow the lead of so many other small towns and wither away. Then two events, both related to the Columbia River, changed the destiny of Hermiston and propelled it pell-mell into the mainstream of progress.

A very large railroad marshaling yard, displaced by the rising waters of the Columbia River and Snake River impoundments, was relocated at Hinkle, a few miles from Hermiston. Overnight, Hermiston gained new prominence and population. Then, irrigation made possible by the new dams on the Columbia arrived in the desert between Hermiston and Boardman, and Hermiston gained new food-processing facilities with attendant commercial and population growth. In a few years, the awakened little town grew out of its original boundaries and started adding street after street of new dwellings, all of which seemed to be occupied before they were fully completed. New businesses, banks, and churches moved in; and today one can get a civilized meal and a decent drink in Hermiston—a somewhat tenuous claim to progress, but one which I have always found valid.

From Umatilla to Boardman, the River feeds various irrigation pumps that move the water inland, sometimes for many miles before it is sprayed from central pivot irrigation sys-

The Middle Columbia is flanked for hundreds of miles with sere brown hills, which are green only in spring.

tems onto a variety of crops that have transformed this section of the Cascadia rain shadow into one of the most fruitful sections of Oregon. Irrigation is not new to this region. Irrigon, a small town betwen Umatilla and Boardman, obviously got its name from an irrigation project, but it never fulfilled its potential until the advent of the dams which made possible not only plenty of water, but cheap and plentiful power with which to pump it. Now, along with the new crops proliferating on formerly useless land, new towns are springing up. Boardman is one of these. Displaced by the rising waters of John Day Dam, Boardman was transplanted to higher ground and given a huge shot of growth hormone by the bountiful produce growing in its back yard. Already, new food-processing plants and allied facilities and housing are spreading out from the town's central core, and busy planning committees burn the midnight kilowatts planning for the growth that is not only assuredly coming but is already here. A few years ago, anyone suggesting that Boardman might some day have a population of ten thousand people would have been considered, to put it kindly, an idealistic dreamer. Today, he would be considered downright conservative and completely unimaginative.

Near Boardman, on land so useless that it has long been used as a naval bombing range, Portland General Electric has built a huge thermal electric plant, fueled by coal shipped in from Wyoming. It is anomalous that a thermal generating plant is a necessity only a few miles from America's most bountiful supplier of electrical energy, but it is indicative of the times. By 1982, when this new coal plant's output was put into the electrical grid, every kilowatt was already spoken for.

Near Arlington, the cliffs begin once more and fringe the river almost all the way to Portland. There are three huge dams in this area: McNary, John Day, and The Dalles, all power-producing units, and each provided with fishways and locks that make slack-water navigation possible all the way to Pasco. This is a very scenic section of the river, with perpendicular basalt cliffs topped by tawny undulating hills that change constantly with the light so that the eye is greeted by an ever-changing panorama. This was the part of the river that Sam Hill, the railroad baron, considered the most beautiful of the whole river, and it is here that he erected an incongruously placed mansion named Mary-

hill, now an endowed museum of the fine arts. Whether he erected and named it for his wife, Mary, the daughter of railroad builder Jim Hill, or his very good friend Marie, queen of Rumania, who dedicated it in 1926, has been the subject of much conjecture, but it remains to this day as a very worthwhile stop, as well as a lasting memorial of this man's love, among other things, of this particularly beautiful stretch of the river.

At Celilo, an Indian longhouse hints that this place may have had some particular significance in the long history of the River. Indeed it has, for while the river smoothly flows behind the impoundment of The Dalles Dam, Celilo Falls, now drowned in thirty feet of slack water, once thundered here. It is always easy to feel, when passing this place, that this is a land haunted by spirits, for this was the center of Indian life for hundreds of miles up and down the river. Here the hated Wishram Indians plied their trade monopoly, exacting tribute from anyone who would pass up and down the River. Here, for untold centuries, Indians netted the mighty chinook salmon that often exhausted themselves in vainly trying to leap the twenty-foot falls. On a stormy night, camped by the river, it is very easy to transmute the crash of thunder and the pounding of storm driven waves into the roar of the falls, and the howling of the strong upriver wind easily becomes the wailing of long departed souls mourning the loss of their ancestral fishing grounds and way of life.

The Dalles, a historic city which played a prominent role in the development of the Northwest, marks the end of the desert country, for it is just within the rain shadow of the nearby Cascades. The River here narrows to only a few hundred feet and is as deep as it is broad. Early travelers sojourned here after the exhausting portage around Celilo Falls and the cascades of Les Dalles ("the narrow places"), and it was a transfer point for goods and passengers during the steamboat era. And indeed, it is an ideal place for a town. The streets climb the hills so that practically everyone has a view, and the town is fittingly crowned by a park.

This was the end of the Old Oregon Trail. From here, the pioneers took boats down the River to the Willamette Valley before the building of the Barstow Road; but judging from the stones still legible in the old Pioneer Cemetery, some of them decided that what they saw right here was the promised land and stayed. The Dalles was chosen as the site of a new mint which would coin the output of the Orofino gold fields, but the strike petered out before the mint could become operative, although the substantial stone walls of the old building still remain.

Today The Dalles is a flourishing small city deriving its living from servicing the adjacent area and the timberlands at its doorstep. On the edge of town, close by the river, is a large aluminum-producing plant operated by Martin-Marietta, utilizing part of the electrical energy produced by The Dalles Dam. A companion plant on the Washington side, some thirty miles upstream, was built in the middle of a field littered with volcanic scoria, illustrating the principle that industry will follow wherever plentiful electrical energy is available, however unfavorable the site otherwise may be.

Downstream from The Dalles, the country changes sharply from a desert to a land of scrub oaks and increasingly taller trees. In twenty miles, the character of the river changes completely: the vegetation becomes increasingly luxuriant, and at Hood River and White Salmon, the hills are clothed in evergreens and the desert river once more becomes a stream flowing through forests reminiscent of those that gave it birth.

Hood River is a fruit-processing center, packing the apples and cherries produced in a long, narrow valley stretching up to the foothills of snowcapped Mount Hood. There is also a distillery there that converts fruit into somewhat more sprightly products, while across the river the town of Bingen, named after a famous German wine town, seeks to emulate its namesake by growing wine grapes on the precipitous slopes edging down to the river.

The famed Columbia Gorge begins just a mile or two downstream from Hood River. This storied area will get a separate chapter, for it is probably the best known scenic attraction on the whole Columbia and deservedly so. The Gorge is one of the scenic wonders of the world: a land of crashing waters, shade-dappled trails, cool glades, and vistas so appealing that the mind becomes surfeit with grandeur and seeks a welcome relief in something as simple as the contemplation of the exquisite symmetry of a lacy fern beaded with moisture blown from an adjacent waterfall.

Halfway down the Gorge stands Bonneville Dam, the grandaddy of the federally built dams on the Columbia. Unlike Grand Coulee Dam, which was built primarily for irrigation with power generation as a secondary consideration, Bonneville was built primarily as a power generation unit and became the prototype on which all future dams were modeled. Just as Grand Coulee Dam is the dividing line between the Upper and Middle River, so Bonneville is the dividing line between the Middle and Lower River. A curious similarity: the Upper River, ending at Grand Coulee Dam, is born in a forested area and ends in a desert; the Middle River, starting in a desert, ends in a forested area. The two stretches of the same river are as different as night is from day, yet they are of the same water. It is only one more facet of this strange, fascinating river which is so diverse in its various parts, so compelling in its entirety.

The Columbia flows on, eager for its mating with the waiting, eternal sea.

The Lower River

THE COLUMBIA RIVER BELOW Bonneville Dam is altogether different in character from the stream that entered the Columbia Gorge some twenty miles to the east. Quieter, flowing with a deep surging flood, it is a stream that has prevailed over five hundred miles of desert, has conquered a mountain range, and now, serene in the knowledge of its power, is content to rest from its labors and flow placidly to the sea. Although it will flow through a mountainous gorge for another fifteen miles, it already is showing the attributes of a tidal river, feeling the ebb and flow of the ocean tides. For the next hundred and twenty miles its progress will be relatively unhurried, as befits a river whose struggle is over and whose destiny it is that it should willingly merge itself with the parent sea.

The River leaves the Columbia Gorge near the town of Washougal, which is approximately the site of Lieutenant Broughton's deepest penetration of the River in 1792. On the Oregon side, the Sandy River, a clear, cold stream draining the snowfields of nearby Mount Hood, is noted for a spring smelt run that brings out thousands of eager fishermen, and clean sandy

The Crown Zellerbach plant at Camas, Washington, is typical of the industry that dominates the Lower River.

beaches on which thousands of nearby Portland's teenagers acquire a golden tan during the summer months. Also, at this stretch of the River the islands begin. Many of the islands of the Upper and Middle Columbia have been swallowed up by the impoundments of the dams that have made most of the Columbia a series of slack-water lakes, but this stretch of the Columbia remains unimpeded on its march to the sea, and the islands that have formed over the centuries are the summer playgrounds of thousands of appreciative visitors who reach them by boat and bask on beaches little changed since the time of Lewis and Clark.

The character of the country has also changed. Instead of the basalt cliffs and sere brown hills topped with wheat fields common only fifty miles upstream, the land shelves down gradually to the river and is covered with a dense forest of fir, alder, and maple. Small streams and rivers enter the main stream at frequent intervals, and the whole landscape indicates that this is a gentle, well-watered land. The air is soft and hazy, with more than a hint of abundant moisture, especially on a warm summer day; and nature responds to these favorable conditions with a wealth of foliage and vegetation positively tropical in its luxuriance. No wonder that many of the pioneers who came down the Columbia by boat concluded that this was the promised land that had lured them on the dangerous trek across the plains and, pulling into shore, put down roots right here rather than chancing the uncertainties of the Willamette Valley which, in their eyes, certainly could be not better than this earthly paradise.

A glance upriver from the vicinity of Camas will reward the viewer with one of the great scenic vistas of the Northwest: Mount Hood, soaring over its kingdom of snow, ice, rock, and forest and proudly surveying a panorama of forest and river equaled in majesty by very few places on this planet. Mount Hood is the dominant mountain in this area, although Mount St. Helens probably is better known. A perfectly symmetrical cone often compared to Japan's Mount Fujiyama, the latter exploded with cataclysmic force on May 18, 1980, devastating hundreds of square miles of timber, causing over seventy deaths, and covering a large part of the Northwest under a carpet of volcanic ash. Today Mount St. Helens is a jagged, broken tooth on the horizon, its symmetry lost. It trails an ominous plume of vapor which constantly reminds the viewer that its volcanic fires, though banked, are far from dead.

The islands are a feature of the Lower River all the way to Astoria. Usually low, with sandy beaches, the smaller ones are generally densely wooded, the larger ones cleared and devoted to agriculture or cattle grazing. The smaller islands are favored picnic and frolicking grounds of the younger set, most of whom seem to either have boats of their own or have access to the family outboard, for on a warm summer day the islands are packed with young people, all of whom have the idea that if they could only get out to an island in the middle of a large river, they'd have a little privacy. Since this idea occurs to thousands of youngsters at the same time, the result is somewhat akin to Coney Island on a weekend, but everyone has a good time anyway.

Because the Columbia has been known to overflow its banks occasionally—there have been some really spectacular floods, especially before the dams on the Middle River were built—a levee fronts the River in the neighborhood of Portland International Airport and continues for miles downstream. Here also are the first clusters of houseboats, a way of life whose fervent devotees claim it represents the finest of all possible lifestyles. Instead of a car in the garage, there is an outboard moored to the front door, the River is a highway, and amphibious children barely able to walk toddle along the edge of the boat wearing life jackets and tethered by long nylon lines.

The Vancouver area, where once the Hudson's Bay Company held sway, is marked by a handsome replica of the early-day post, complete with palisade and ancient cannons. The historic town of Vancouver is full of mementoes of its colorful past—the old brick buildings of the fort the U.S. Army maintained here for many years, a pioneer Catholic school and hospital—as well as the appurtenances of a modern city, for Vancouver is alive, well, and growing. There are also many river-oriented businesses along the banks: one can see everything from barge line terminals busily forming the tows that will ply the Lower and Middle River, to offshore drilling rigs under construction. And all along the River, half hidden by giant firs, are handsome homes whose large picture windows look out over an ever-changing panorama of activity along this vital artery of the Northwest.

The Interstate Bridge between Portland and Vancouver carries an impressive burden of traffic which may be interrupted when an ocean freighter or a particularly tall barge demands passage up or down river. Downstream from the bridge, the River is lined for miles by industrial plants, practically all of which depend on it one way or another. The River, which in its upper stretches busied itself spinning turbines to generate electrical energy, now carries on its broad back the produce of that same energy and helps disseminate it to the markets of the world.

Six miles below Vancouver, after threading its way through islands, the Willamette steals into the Columbia. This is the second largest of the Columbia's tributaries, second in volume only to the Snake, but it drains the most densely populated part of the Columbia River basin and touches the three largest cities in Oregon. The Willamette also has another mark of distinction: it is probably the largest river in the United States that from an ecological standpoint has been successfully rehabilitated. Only fifteen years ago, no one swam in the Willamette if he could help it. It was a turgid, polluted stream in which only the strongest fish barely survived: an open sewer heavy with the effluent of paper mills, manufacturing plants, and untreated sewage. This beautiful stream, flowing through one of the most enchanting valleys in the country, was in its worst stretches a stinking cesspool, heavy with algae and seemingly incapable of ever again becoming the crystal clear mountain stream that springs from the Cascades and Coast Range. Then, public outcry made possible the application of stringent laws that resulted in a massive clean-up program. Today, trout teem in its upper reaches, and a successfully replanted salmon run provides fishermen with legendary sport as far as the falls of Oregon City. Around Eugene, Corvallis, Albany, and Salem, the Willamette is once more an aquatic playground, a source of pleasure to the thousands of people whose lives are considerably enriched by the presence of a stream that is once more clear, sparkling, enjoyable water. The rehabilitation of the Willamette was accomplished only at great cost to industry and municipalities alike, but anyone enjoying the lazy stretches of this beautiful stream on a warm summer afternoon will tell you that the price was not excessive, considering what it bought.

Eugene, situated near the head of the Willamette, is the second largest city in Oregon. A pleasant, bustling city growing much too fast for the tastes of many of its inhabitants, it is the home of the University of Oregon and, along with neighboring Springfield, the center of Oregon's wood-products industry. Numerous paper and wood-products plants provide solid bases for its industrial strength, while the presence of the University brings to the city the amenities attendant to a seat of learning. In spite of the ubiquitous rain, life is very good in Eugene, which has somewhat blended the advantages of a metropolitan center with the charm of a small town. Maybe that's why the city is growing so fast, although there are other reasons, not the least of which is the availability of comparatively unspoiled wilderness only a few minutes from the busy center of the city.

Thirty miles downstream, the Willamette flows past Corvallis, the seat of Oregon State University. A pretty, tree-shaded college town, it readily admits to being dominated by the University—and counts its blessings. Education, the inhabitants will tell you, is here to stay, and that's Corvallis's business. Here the Willamette is the training ground for the University's eight-oared shells, and the sight of these graceful boats knifing through the waters of the river makes one very glad that the stream has been cleaned up enough to make the coxswain's traditional victory dunking something other than a punishment.

Ten miles down the river is another kind of town. Albany's present and future is centered as much in industry as Corvallis's is in education. A busy, energetic town, the site of the famous Timber Carnival, it fairly bursts with activity. Evidently some of the best brains educated at Oregon State University could see opportunity here, for Albany is the center of the exotic metal industry in Oregon. It bills itself as a city of opportunity, and indeed it is, if one has the brains and stamina to withstand the high-powered competition that is inevitably attracted to a thriving, well-entrenched industrial center.

Still farther down the Willamette is Oregon's capitol city, Salem. The government of a state as dynamic as Oregon is big business, and Salem tends to it very well. Like most of the towns along the Willamette, Salem is a pretty place with well-laid-out, tree-shaded streets in the better residential districts; and through it the river threads its way, a special delight to anyone fortunate enough to have a home fronting on it. Salem does more than govern the state: it also is an important retail and manufacturing center, especially in forest products and related industries.

At Oregon City, the Willamette, after having meandered through an idyllically beautiful valley, kicks up its heels for the last time before it merges with the Columbia. The falls in the river were early exploited as a source of water power, so that Oregon City was actually one of the first places in the Valley to have a substantial white population. Today, a dam holds back the river, but the falls still occasionally thunder in their old accustomed way, and the mills along the edge of the river don't seem to inhibit the salmon one bit as they try to jump the falls, just as had their ancestors for thousands of years.

Most of the river below Oregon City is fronted by homes, all the way to Portland, where the Willamette finally feels the pull of the tide and fulfills its destiny. The Willamette made possible Portland, the pearl of the Northwest, and certainly one of the most intriguing and delightfully located cities in America. In a recent poll conducted by a large survey organization, Portland was adjudged to have the best quality of life of any large city in the United States. This certainly was no surprise to Portlanders, who had always known that their city provided them with numerous advantages, any one of which would have been a major bragging point for any other place.

The story of how Portland was so named on the toss of a coin by Francis Pettygrove, a native of Portland, Maine (rather than the "Boston" favored by his friend Amos Lovejoy) is well known, but the reasons underlying its growth are somewhat more obscure. Portland was favored over the already well established Vancouver not only because of a sandbar, since removed, that inhibited passage to Vancouver for large oceangoing vessels, but also because it was founded by canny New Englanders who were well established in the shipping fraternity and who had enough vision to see in these hills and plains covered by a veritable jungle of rain forest the makings of a great city. They also weren't above exploiting their friendships with other skippers to see to it that their investment grew and prospered.

The original settler of Portland was William Overton, who was soon bought out by a group of mariners intrigued by the fact that the Willamette at this point was deep enough to bring oceangoing ships close to shore, an ideal

Portland at dusk, from Vista Avenue.

The Willamette River, now rehabilitated to its original clarity, meanders for miles through a valley often compared to that of the Thames. This scene, near Corvallis, Oregon, could be from an English countryside.

spot for wharves and warehouses. John T. Couch, a respected mariner who later acquired large holdings in what is now Northwest Portland, stated: "To this point I can bring any ship that can get into the mouth of the Columbia River, and no farther." He was wrong, but the statement had much to do with locating the city where it is, and in view of how well it turned out, he may be forgiven if his remark was somewhat less than the whole truth.

One should remember that at this time the American domination of the Oregon Territory, though not complete, was well under way, and the founding of a new city at Portland may well have been aimed at overcoming the last vestiges of British domination at Vancouver, as well as founding an American bastion of impeccable lineage. Undoubtedly, the main aim of the founders was economic: they saw a chance to get in on the ground floor of a very good thing, although any benefit that would accrue to their country was viewed as a welcome – but secondary – bonus.

For a few years after its founding, downtown Portland was still dotted with huge stumps – whitewashed for better visibility at night – and was very much a rudimentary frontier town. Then gold was discovered in California and overnight the timber that up to then had been a nuisance best disposed of by burning became a commodity for which the Forty-Niners were willing to exchange good hard cash or equally negotiable gold dust. The rush was on, and in a few years Portland grew into a busy, rowdy frontier boom town, with garish saloons and bordellos fronting the Willamette. Timber was king . . . and Portland became its port of egress to the world.

That deep moorage on the Willamette began to prove its worth. Lumber schooners would tie up at the dock, fill their holds with the sloppily finished lumber Portland was producing from its crude mills, tie on a monstrous deck load, and then take a chance at running the Columbia Bar without capsizing or losing their topside loads. One good trip could make the skipper a fortune, and several trips could provide the capital that would build the mills and mansions of the lumber barons who were to dominate the economy of the Northwest for the greater part of a century. Many of those mansions were built in Portland, for certainly few cities are as favorably situated. From the heights overlooking the city's central core, one

is treated to a panorama of the river and streets spreading out to the horizon, while in the distance Mount Hood grows roseate in the glow of twilight, and the city below becomes a fairyland of twinkling lights as night approaches.

Portland, especially the western part, is a city of hills, parks, and views. Parts of it densely wooded, it still retains many of the attributes of a small town, which it definitely is not. Portland is a major cosmopolitan city, one of the main gates to the Orient, and a vital, growing metropolitan center. It prospers because it is well situated to serve the needs of a growing region, and because the river at its front door provides a highway to the sea and to the world. The skyscrapers and high-rise buildings that are proliferating in its rehabilitated downtown area proclaim this to be a center of commerce and industry, yet only a half hour away, one can sleep under a canopy of primeval forest firs, beside a noisy mountain stream that is completely potable. Not many major cities in the world can make that claim.

Portland has grown to the point that it now fronts on the Columbia as well as on the Willamette, and both streams provide it with transportation and recreation. The Willamette below Portland is solid with industry, and busy tugs ply the waters night and day, moving everything from an incoming freighter to a raft of logs a quarter of a mile long. A major ship repair station is maintained at Swan Island, and the Port of Portland every year sees its tonnage records exceeded. Maybe those old New Englanders who chose the site of Portland didn't estimate the navigational potential of the Willamette that well, but when it came to picking city sites, they were in a class by themselves.

The Columbia River below the mouth of the Willamette is still bounded by low, marshy country with numerous sloughs and islands. One of these islands, Sauvie, is mentioned by Lewis and Clark as a favorite spot of the Indians for potlatches, a sort of gift-giving celebration whereby one Indian would bankrupt himself giving presents to his contemporaries, hoping to recoup his fortune when it became his turn to be on the receiving end. Sauvie Island today is prime agricultural land, protected from the river by strong dikes and supporting herds of cows that provide Portland with a large part of its dairy supplies.

Kalama, Washington, a small town on the Columbia, once had aspirations of becoming the western terminus of a transcontinental railroad and for a short time became a boom town. The boom went bust when Tacoma got the honor, and now Kalama busies itself as a port. From Interstate Highway 5 there is also a very good view of the cooling tower of Oregon's only nuclear electrical generation facility at Rainier, towering above the wooded landscape like an incongruously placed giant spittoon.

Also at Rainier, the river is bridged by a graceful high steel bridge extending to the outskirts of Longview, Washington. This is a comparatively new town, founded in 1927 by the Long-Bell Lumber Company. A completely planned company town, it was laid out with the idea of keeping natural beauty and enhancing, rather than destroying, the natural environment. The world's largest integrated lumber mill fronts the Columbia for over a mile, incorporating in an extremely modern facility technological developments that utilize every single part of a log and keep the air and water clean while doing it. Longview is a city completely devoted to the forest products industry, and it prospers mightily with it.

Downstream from Longview with its line of docks, the River is again edged by cliffs as it cuts through a low part of the Coast Range. Here are little towns—Cathlamet, Wauna, Bradwood—mostly devoted to logging and milling, but increasingly as the mouth of the River is neared, geared to fishing. Also, for the first time, one begins to see the remains of old canneries and villages that have died with the decline of the fishing industry in the River. The islands become lower, more marshy and, with the exception of Puget Island near the mouth, undeveloped. Puget Island is of considerable size, with a network of sloughs, and is used mostly for grazing.

The River splits into many sloughs in this area, a sure sign that the mouth is near. Then it suddenly opens up into a bay some eight or ten miles wide, and in the hazy distance mountains can be seen with a distinct break between them. The air becomes fresher, with a salty tang to it, and it is obvious that the union with the ocean is near. Then, at last, one rounds a wooded point and there it is! To the left, a city surmounted by a tall column—Astoria—crowds down to the water's edge. Soaring in a high, graceful arc over the river, a steel bridge frames an expanse of water with no visible shore.

One can at last fully appreciate Clark's entry in his diary when he inscribed with more fervor than good spelling "Ocian in view, Oh, the joy!" It is still some miles before the Bar is reached, but this can be called the River's end. Here the drop of water that originally crept down the side of a Canadian mountain to become part of the nascent Columbia River finally meets the ocean, for from here one can see, smell, and taste salt water.

The Columbia has attained its purpose and become once more part of the sea from which it primarily sprang.

Journey's end.

Giant
in
Chains

IN THE WHOLE OF THE Columbia River's twelve hundred and sixty-four miles of length, less than three hundred miles run freely. Over nine hundred miles of this, North America's most powerful river, are constrained in steel and concrete chains that effectively bend the River to the needs of man and force it to do his will.

That puny man could tame such an elemental force and turn it to his bidding is one of the greatest engineering accomplishments in the history of civilization: one that has drastically altered the character of the River and profoundly influenced the lives of those who live within its domain. In less than half a century, the giant river which had for eons obeyed no law other than that of Nature found itself tamed, shackled, and made into a more or less obedient servant of man. But it must be remembered that while the Columbia is a tamed giant, it also has on occasion demonstrated its ability to throw off its bonds and revert to the wild elemental force it had been before man bound it in shackles of steel and concrete. It may be a chained giant, but it is nevertheless a natural

Bonneville Dam, the first federally funded, multipurpose dam on the Columbia, is still an important part of the power generating and navigational complex on the Lower Columbia.

force of frightening proportions and one that knowledgeable persons always treat with a respect commensurate with its strength.

Although man had been utilizing the power of falling water as a source of energy for centuries, the early Northwest pioneers showed little or no interest in harnessing the awesome force of the Columbia. They looked upon the big river as a highway and turned to the more amenable smaller streams for their energy requirements. As early as 1846 Dr. John McLoughlin had utilized part of the falls of the Willamette at Oregon City to grind corn and saw lumber, but the Columbia apparently was considered too big to harness, even by the doughty pioneers to whom any other challenge was only something meant to be surmounted. It wasn't until the twentieth century, when technological advances coincided with social and economic needs, that man was able to assert his mastery over the River, for like any good idea, it had to wait for the proper time and place.

The time came in 1933, when the government of a nation in the throes of a worldwide depression saw in the Grand Coulee Project a program big enough to give heavy industry a badly needed shot in the arm, provide jobs for thousands of unemployed workers, and capture the imagination of a nation sadly in need of some good news.

As early as 1918, Rufus Wood, the crusading publisher of the *Wenatchee World,* had been pushing the idea of his friend, Billy Clapp, an Ephrata lawyer, to dam the Columbia at the site of an Ice Age ice barrier, divert part of the flow into the ancient bed of the Columbia, the Grand Coulee, provide "power as great as another Niagara," and irrigate a million acres of arid land that with water could be transformed into some of the most productive farmland in the nation.

He found his man in Franklin Delano Roosevelt, a man with enough imagination and daring to see the possibilities of what many considered a completely visionary scheme. Accustomed as we are today to seeing Grand Coulee Dam and the Columbia Basin Project as highly successful, functioning entities, it may come as some surprise to learn that both projects were bitterly opposed. Why build a huge power plant in the middle of a blighted Western desert? Who'd use the power? Jackrabbits? "Why," said one opponent, "if you electrified every gopher hole in Eastern Washington, you still couldn't use all that juice."

As for the irrigation scheme, opponents could rightly point out that several dozen schemes to irrigate this same desert had been proposed, some even put into effect, and all had failed. This one, they said, was different only in that the failure would be on a much larger scale.

Then, too, there were vague presentiments that when government began building projects heretofore reserved for private enterprise, it meant the thin edge of the entering wedge that would some day split the capitalistic system. Socialism and communism were often equated, and many dire predictions were made that the concrete giant rising in the bed of the Columbia was the first monument to a new era.

In a way, it was. The Bonneville and Grand Coulee projects on the Columbia and the Tennessee Valley project in the South ushered in a new era of federal control over natural resources. In view of the good working relationship the government has achieved with private enterprise, it must be conceded it was a good idea. Certainly, these projects would never have been created by a private industry almost laid prostrate by the Great Depression.

While Roosevelt was still a presidential candidate, he had outlined to the nation a plan aimed at developing natural resources and promoting jobs. True to his campaign promises, he actively supported the idea proposed by Billy Clapp in 1918, and on September 3, 1933, the stakes for the axis of the dam were driven.

The building of the Grand Coulee Dam is a saga in itself. Into the desert poured an army of workers, lured by the magic of jobs at the princely sum of fifty cents an hour. At first housed in tents, lean-tos, or anything that provided the most rudimentary shelter, they almost overnight built the towns of Electric City, Grand Coulee, and Mason City. Prostitutes flocked in to serve the thousands of lonely workers, and bars and brothels doing a roaring twenty-four-hours-a-day business more successfully recreated the atmosphere of a nineteenth-century gold camp than anything since the Klondike.

The bars weren't the only things going twenty-four hours a day. Under glaring sun or glaring floodlights, concrete was poured, the river channel was juggled from side to side, and individual columns of concrete were fused into the monolithic giant that today spans the Columbia. New processes were invented on the spot, for there were no precedents on a job of this size. A mountain of sliding clay was frozen into immobility and the heat of the setting concrete dissipated by thousands of miles of refrigerating pipes still embedded in the giant dam's framework. Eighty-nine men were to lose their lives in the construction of this dam, but theirs is as imposing a monument as exists on the face of this planet. The technologies developed in the building of Grand Coulee were to become standard throughout the industry, for no major dam today is built without leaning on the expertise developed during those days of industrial pioneering. Grand Coulee Dam is not only a technical achievement of the first water, but also a triumph of the human spirit over seemingly impossible odds.

Whie the original plan for Grand Coulee had called for a low dam, this soon was changed to a high dam with two powerhouses, housing the largest generators then in existence. These were originally rated at 108,000 kilowatts but have since been rewound to 125,000-kilowatt capacity. Proponents of this tremendous electrical output were of the opinion that industries using huge amounts of electrical energy, such as chemical or aluminum reduction plants, would follow cheap energy sources and that the Northwest would in time absorb whatever energy could be produced in the region from whatever source. They would quietly smile today, were they to see the third powerhouse at Coulee Dam, whose six gargantuan generators have a combined output greater than that of the original eighteen . . . and whose every single kilowatt is either committed even before it is produced or will be needed within the next few years.

The first power from Grand Coulee went "on the line" March 22, 1941 when two small 10,000-kilowatt generators were activated by Chief Jim James of the Nez Percé Indian tribe. That activation was symbolic, for while the energy produced by these two small supplemental generators flowed to the nearby Colville Indian Reservation, it also was generated by water in a reservoir that would soon swallow the grave sites of Indians who for centuries had buried their dead on the banks of the Columbia. But at last, Grand Coulee was finally working, and in October 1941 the first of the 108,000-kilowatt generators was activated and power pulsed over the lines to the towns and cities of the Northwest.

Grand Coulee couldn't have been built at a better price or completed at a better time. Built during a depression when wages and material prices were at the lowest ebb in decades, it was a fantastic bargain that couldn't be duplicated today at twenty times the price. And its huge blocs of power came onto the market just as America faced its needs for aluminum to build fifty thousand warplanes and electricity to fuel a massive war effort. Grand Coulee made possible the Flying Fortresses that spearheaded the Allied drive into Europe and reduced Hitler's "Thousand Year Reich" to a burned, blackened ruin. Down the river, huge blocs of Grand Coulee power were going to a highly secret installation at Hanford whose purpose was unknown until incandescent fireballs over Hiroshima and Nagasaki spelled the doom of the Japanese Empire, the end of World War II, and the birth of the Atomic Age.

Though the skeptics who had wondered what was going to happen to all that electrical power generated by Grand Coulee were temporarily silenced, they nodded knowingly and said, "Wait till the war is over. What will you do with a million surplus kilowatts when there are no more war industries to run?"

The answer came within three years. By that time, even with additional generating capacity installed and producing, the Northwest was using every available kilowatt and begging for more. The people who had claimed that industry would flock to a place with abundant electrical power turned out to be first-class prophets, and a rapidly growing region with people to whom a houseful of electrical gadgetry was simply a normal way of life was creating a shortage in what had been, only a decade ago, a colossal surplus. The Northwest had become the most thoroughly electrified part of the whole country—a distinction it has never surrendered. Grand Coulee and the other dams that were shortly to follow it on the Columbia and its tributaries can take a lot of credit for that, for the power generated here is the least expensive in the country, a fact which has led to wholesale electrical living and lured to this region a host of industries thriving on cheap electrical energy.

Grand Coulee was not the first dam on the Columbia to generate electrical energy: that distinction is usually awarded to Rock Island, which first produced commercial power in 1933. As early as 1908, a canal around Priest Rapids had spun two generators which continued to

The generation room at Wanapum Dam, on the Columbia, built by Oregon's Grant County Public Utilities District.

John Day Dam, on the Columbia, was built by the U.S. Army Corps of Engineers, Walla Walla District.

produce power for local consumption as late as 1957, when the present Priest Rapids Dam engulfed the power site. Nevertheless, Grand Coulee, by virtue of its sheer, staggering size and dramatic role in the development of the Northwest, has captured public imagination to the point that when the Columbia River is mentioned, most people automatically think of Grand Coulee.

IT IS NOT AT ALL UNUSUAL for people seeing Grand Coulee Dam for the first time to be somewhat disappointed. They have heard of its huge size, the fact that it is the world's largest monolithic concrete structure, and they are somewhat disappointed that it doesn't seem bigger. Then, the tour guide may mention that those ports in the face of the dam that look like arrow slits on a medieval castle are actually sixty feet long and that the tiny box crawling along the top of the dam is really a twenty-ton, eighteen-wheel truck. . . . and the massive size of this huge structure begins to sink in.

Actually, eight pyramids each the size of the Great Pyramid of Cheops could be placed side by side along the face of the dam with room to spare, and they would not tower as high above the surface of the river as does the crest of the dam. Grand Coulee is not simply big, it is staggeringly huge and its size doesn't penetrate the viewer's consciousness until he has spent a day or so tramping through its galleries and walking along apparently interminable corridors that make a concrete honeycomb of this seemingly monolithic structure.

When Grand Coulee Dam was first envisioned, the engineers figured that the eighteen generators provided in the first design would be adequate for at least half a century. At 108,000-kilowatt nameplate rating each, these generators were the largest then in existence. Within two years after completion, however, the total output of the dam was being used, and the new dams coming on the line on the middle river were barely keeping up with the demands of a rapidly growing region that used vast quantities of electrical energy in its new industries and in every phase of its everyday life. And so the need for the third powerhouse came into being.

Electrical energy, for all its usefulness and adaptability, has one huge drawback: once produced, it cannot be stored. The minimal flow of the Columbia, run through the turbines of the dams on the mainstream, can be depended on to produce a steady base flow of electrical energy. This, coupled with the usually steady, preferably unvarying output of thermal plants is called *base load* and is ordinarily equal to the basic requirements of the region served by those plants. At certain times of the day, such as at breakfast, when many electrical utensils are simultaneously turned on and factories begin their daily runs, or evening, when millions of TV tubes are activated, demand for electrical energy escalates. The demands of these "peak use" periods are best met by hydroelectric generators which can be activated simply by opening the gate on a turbine, utilizing water dammed up for just such a purpose. This is the reason that the river flow below a large dam varies so much: there probably will be some generators running at all times, and this maintains normal river flow; but during peak periods all generators may be running and the flow of the river will be considerably enhanced. The erratic flow must be regulated by another dam, and for this, as well as many other reasons, one dam alone on a river cannot do an efficient job. A whole series of dams, tied into one another by computer so that each downriver dam is in effect a reregulating dam, efficiently smooths out the peaks and valleys of the river's flow and functions as one integral unit, which in effect is exactly what it is.

All the dams on the Columbia, from Mica to Bonneville, are tied together into one smoothly functioning unit by centrally located computers, which do much "talking" between themselves. Thus, water released from Mica is effectively monitored all the way down to Bonneville, spinning turbines and controlling the passage of anadromous fish all the way to tidewater. With the system tied together as a whole, the storage capacity of any dam on the river effectively becomes the sum of all the impoundments above it. While Coulee is the only United States dam on the Columbia with any significant storage capacity, the other dams on the mainstream are *run-of-the-river* dams, which mainly depend on stream flow for their generating capacity. That this flow can be regulated from the huge impoundments in Mica and Arrow Lakes reservoirs becomes of tremendous importance, and this is what made possible the new third powerhouse at Grand Coulee which

once more restored to that dam the position of the world's largest supplier of electrical energy, a place temporarily ceded to the Soviet Union's giant plant at Krasnoyarsk, on the Yenisey River.

Although the unregulated Columbia by its very nature is a prime power-producing stream, it really did not hit its peak of efficiency till the 1964 Columbia River Treaty with Canada went into effect. This treaty provided for three dams in Canada: Mica and Arrow Lakes (now Keenleyside Dam) on the mainstream Columbia and Duncan on a tributary of the Kootenay. It also provided for a storage near Libby Dam, on the Kootenai in the United States, which backs up water some forty miles into Canada. (Incidentally, this is the same river, but the spelling is Kootenai in the United States and Kootenay in Canada.) The combined storage capacities of these dams is large enough to contain the seasonal peaks of the river, providing flood control and utilizing those peaks for power generation during periods of reduced flow. While Canada has only 15 percent of the total drainage area of the Columbia, it contributes almost 30 percent of its flow; thus the large storage reservoirs behind the Columbia dams not only tamed the wild spring floods which formerly wreaked havoc downstream, but also stored enough water to guarantee at least 2.8 million kilowatts of dependable power. A large part of this power goes to Southern California over the Pacific Northwest – Southern California Intertie, a very complex, highly sophisticated two-way street for electrical energy. Power generated during the high flow periods in the summer goes south to feed the voracious irrigation pumps and air conditioners of Southern California and is returned during the Northwest's periods of low generation by energy produced in California's thermal plants. This dependable supply of water, coupled with a steady market for huge blocs of power, is one of the factors that makes the third powerhouse at Coulee Dam a mechanical and economic feasibility.

The Canadian treaty not only made it possible for Canada to share in the hydrological

This scene, at the edge of the third powerhose at Grand Coulee Dam, had best be viewed from the photograph. Perpetually drenched in spray, the rocks are very slippery and extremely dangerous.

bounty of the Columbia—for it shares in the additional power generated as a result of the treaty—but by guaranteeing an adequate supply of water downstream from the huge impoundments in British Columbia also made possible many new generators. However, these provisions could not be implemented until adequate supplies of water could be guaranteed. With the Canadian treaty in effect, additional generators have been added from Grand Coulee to Bonneville . . . and their added output is immediately absorbed by the seemingly insatiable demands of a power-hungry region. The supply may not always be up to the demand, but at least, with the added capacity, the Columbia comes closer to meeting its hydrological potential.

The Grand Coulee and Bonneville dams were built largely as economic measures during the Great Depression, but their worth soon became so apparent that other federal projects inevitably followed. At the dedication of McNary Dam, President Dwight D. Eisenhower publicly committed the government to a policy of partnership with private industry whose purpose would be the development of the Columbia for the public good. Three huge new federal dams on the mainstream, Chief Joseph, The Dalles, and John Day, soon followed. Near Wenatchee, a very active Chelan County Public Utilities District (PUD) built Rocky Reach and enlarged Rock Island, while downstream Grant County PUD built Wanapum and Priest Rapids. By 1967, Douglas County PUD had built Wells Dam, the last dam on the Columbia with fish ladders; and thus the whole American sector of the Columbia from the Canadian border to tidewater, save for a seventy-mile stretch above Hanford, became a series of slack-water pools.

The River was effectively chained.

In a project of this size, there is bound to be a difference of opinion as to whether this achievement is desirable. A majority, citing the advantages of abundant electrical energy, flood control, ease of navigation, and irrigation benefits, think it is. A small but vociferous minority who apparently would prefer keeping the Columbia a wild river running untrammeled to the sea, disagree. The mid 1960s saw the formation of many ecologically oriented groups to whom nature and abundant hunting and fishing apparently were more important than jobs, development, and the abundant energy our society takes so much for granted without too much thought of whence it originates. Admittedly a minority, they nevertheless wield an influence out of all proportion to their numbers but serve a useful purpose as a brake on the ambitions of those who would completely subvert the character of the river and reduce it solely to an instrument of power, transportation, and irrigation.

Whether or not a majority of the people agree that the regulation of the Columbia as an overall project is desirable, it really is a moot question. It is here and it is here to stay. Those concrete barriers across the river were designed for a practically unlimited lifetime and, barring technological achievements that would make their removal desirable, probably will still be regulating the flow of the Columbia for centuries to come.

Modern industrial technology has greatly improved the efficiency of the turbines and generators used to produce electrical energy. New, low-profile turbines specifically adapted to work efficiently with a low head are marvelously adapted to the Columbia's flow and are generally supplanting the old-style turbines which need massive quantities of water to function properly. The Bonneville Power Administration (BPA), which distributes and markets the power produced by the river dams, has pioneered new, efficient methods of transporting huge amounts of electrical energy for long distances with minimal loss and is in the forefront of a research program aimed at making a good system even better. With the advent of different methods of transmitting power, most likely by laser or microwaves, the tall transmission towers of the BPA may someday disappear; for the time being, they are an ubiquitous reminder that power generated on the Columbia heats, lights, and powers a large part of the country and plays a decisive role in the development of the Northwest.

While the dams on the mainstream Columbia, by virtue of their dramatic size and output, capture the public imagination, it should be remembered that a very significant portion of the total power load in the Columbia River basin is generated on tributaries of the main river. The Kootenai, near Libby, Montana, presently generates 420 megawatts and will be developed to 840, while the lower stretches of the Kootenay, in Canada, are harnessed by five low dams owned by Cominco, the giant mining and smelting conglomerate, which generate an undisclosed but certainly impressive amount of power. The metallurgical plant at Trail, the world's largest smelter of lead and zinc ores, uses the output of these dams in processes which by their very nature consume enormous amounts of electrical energy. The Pend Oreille, once one of the wildest white-water rivers in the Northwest, now is a series of placid pools behind a whole series of high dams. This river, after running the greater part of its length in the United States, barely qualifies as a Canadian tributary of the Columbia by thundering into the main river a scant seventy-five yards north of the forty-ninth parallel.

Next to the Columbia, the most prolific purveyor of power in the Northwest is the Snake River, with four major dams from its mouth to the Idaho border. These dams—Ice Harbor, Lower Monumental, Little Goose, and Lower Granite—were all built in a twenty-year span and not only made the tributary an impressive source of electrical energy, but also made Lewiston Idaho's only seaport.

Engineers eyeing the precipitous walls of Hell's Canyon have long felt that here would be the ideal site for a high dam utilizing the tremendous force of water pouring through this scenic wonder. It would also effectively drown out one of the most beautiful spots on this continent. Much as the power is needed, anyone familiar with Hell's Canyon and appreciative of its splendors would agree that in the inevitable tradeoff that accompanies the building of a high dam, this time the emphasis should be on beauty. Alternative sources of energy can and will be found, but Hell's Canyon is unique and should be preserved as a wild river, so that generations yet unborn may someday enjoy the sight of a river still fresh from the hands of its Creator.

Once the Columbia has breached the Cascades, the fall of the river noticeably decreases, as does its energy-producing potential. One of the Columbia's main tributaries, the Willamette, usually pictured as meandering through an idyllic valley, nevertheless has several dams on its upper reaches, tributaries that feed an im-

pressive amount of power into the Northwest power grid and have much to do with keeping the thriving cities of the valley heated, lighted, and growing.

And so it is throughout the whole Columbia River system. From the wild reaches of the Big Bend to the snowy escapments of the Tetons, the force of the River and its tributaries has been artificially shaped and controlled so that the Columbia River flows on its way to the sea a servant of man. That it is a sometimes unruly and always an unwilling servant is a well-known fact, as the Teton Dam disaster will attest. Nevertheless, the fact remains that the high water of 1964, a potential disaster, was so effectively contained by the dams on the Columbia and its tributaries that most people were unaware that any problem even existed. A lesser volume of water in 1948 on the then largely uncontrolled river smashed Vanport into a muddy ruin.

A great river is an artery through which the life blood of a region courses, and the Columbia is undoubtedly the jugular of the whole Pacific Northwest. The fact that it is a controlled river, with much of its scenic wildness subdued, may cause a few twinges of nostalgia for the beauty that was, but weighed against the manifold benefits provided by the controlled river, it must be admitted that the changes have been beneficial to the great majority of the people whose lives it affects. The chains are still new and the galls still show, but in time they will become an accepted part of the river, as natural as the rockslides which, for centuries before man began changing its face, changed the littoral of the living stream and in time became a natural and accepted part of the River's life.

So it is with the dams controlling the River's flow. To generations yet unborn they will seem a normal and natural part of the river and be counted not as chains binding a restive giant, but as normal accouterments of a friendly and beneficial stream that through many years of service to man has become that greatest of all treasures, a great and trusted friend.

Miracle in the Sun

TO THE WEARY TRAVELERS of the Oregon Trail, hostile Indians, enervating heat, poisonous snakes, bitter water, and spoiled, monotonous food were expected and stoically borne nuisances: part of the necessary hazards that must be endured if ever they were to reach the lush meadows of the Promised Land. But even as they dreamed of the rich soils of the Willamette Valley, they cursed the fine dust raised in choking clouds by the plodding hooves of their slowly moving oxen. In the journals of the pioneers, the dust is most often mentioned as the supreme aggravation of a highly uncomfortable journey. It engendered a hatred of the desert that was to last a lifetime, long after the other discomforts had been forgotten or romanticized.

It probably never dawned on those settlers that that choking dust could be transformed into the rich dark loam of their fondest dreams. Given water, many desert soils, which have never suffered the leaching action of frequent rains and are therefore rich in minerals, can be-

These huge pipes carry irrigation water from the lake behind Coulee Dam to Banks Lake, where it flows by gravity to the canals of the Columbia Basin Project.

come superlatively good farmlands and raise prodigious crops. Probably nowhere in in the Columbia River Basin is the delicate balance that Nature requires for productive land better exemplified than in the semiarid desert formed by the rain-shadow of the Cascades.

Before food grains or vegetables can be grown, certain elements must be present: sunshine, fertile soil, and sufficient water. Take any one away and plants wither and die, unless centuries of adaptation have acclimated them to an inhospitable habitat. The broad plains of Central Oregon and Washington have plenty of sunshine, often deep and fertile soil, but only in isolated oases is there sufficient life-giving water. And so, millions of acres, usually covered with a luxuriant growth of sagebrush, were bypassed by settlers on their way to the well-watered lands of the Pacific slope. Such lands were considered worthless and the few settlers who tried to farm them usually starved to death or gave up in a few years, leaving behind a pathetic legacy of broken-down shacks and rusting machinery to attest to the fact that sunshine and fertile soils were not enough. The life-blood of such lands is water, and without it, the land will inevitably defeat anyone attempting to till it, even if he waters it liberally with his own sweat.

There is a popular myth, partly fostered by the early settlers eager to justify their takeover of Indian lands, that the white man introduced irrigation to the Northwest. This simply does not stand the test of impartial research. Along with the Zunis, the Hopis, and other tribes of the Far West, the Kawachin Indians of the Northwest practiced irrigation, albeit on a comparatively small scale. The fact that the practice was not too widely used arises from the natural pragmatism of the red man. Why kill yourself farming, even if the squaws did all the work, when the nearby rivers teemed with fish? And so the Cayuse were merely amused when Marcus Whitman showed them how to irrigate crops in the Walla Walla Valley. That comparatively well watered region did not afford as spectacular a showcase as did the Yakima. The early Jesuit missionaries there showed that the arid, often stony land of the Yakima Valley, given water, could grow just about anything but tropical plants and fruits. Wenatchee apples, already well established on the banks of the Columbia, were helped along by a canal that brought the waters of the Wenatchee River to

uplands previously considered worthless, but which suddenly blossomed with magnificent orchards once the water arrived. Wherever the water could be applied, the land fructified and showed what could be possible if it could be irrigated on a large scale.

The advent of the railroads, with the access they provided for foodstuffs to the large markets of the East Coast and Midwest, spurred many irrigation developments. Very few prospered, since the cost of pumping and distributing water was simply more than the meagerly financed projects could bear. For years, forests of dead fruit trees, deserted farms, and broken-down windmills remained as testimonials that the desert is an implacable adversary which yields its riches only grudgingly. The moribund, dusty little towns of the Columbia Basin, almost all of which had a peculiar unfinished look, hung on only because of the stubbornness of the people who had founded them, and exported mostly a crop of young men and women who departed as soon as they became of age, seeking greener, better watered fields.

That was the scene in 1918 when Rufus Wood, publisher of the *Wenatchee World*, visited his friend Billy Clapp in Ephrata and put in motion a plan that was to result fifteen years later in the Grand Coulee Project. For years, people around Ephrata had known that the Columbia, dammed by an Ice Age glacier near the present location of Grand Coulee Dam, had formed a new channel down the Grand Coulee, ripped out a new river bed, and returned to its original channel only when the ice dam had melted. Clapp's scheme, the feasibility of which was soon verified by professional engineers, was to dam the Columbia at approximately the location of that ancient ice dam, close the Grand Coulee by dams at either end, and pump water from the reservoir behind the dam into the resulting lake, whence it could be distributed by gravity flow to over a million formerly arid acres.

It should be remembered that this Coulee Dam project was originally conceived as an irrigation measure, with power definitely a secondary consideration. World War II, with its needs for massive blocs of electrical energy, changed all that. During and immediately after the war years, the emphasis was on power production, since new industries attracted by the cheap and plentiful electrical energy of the

Columbia River dams sprang up almost overnight. But eventually, emphasis shifted back to the primary reason that implemented the original project: irrigation. However, the two products of the Coulee Dam—water for irrigation and electrical energy—are so inextricably bound together that they must be considered as an entity. In effect, the Columbia River is made to lift itself by its own bootstraps, for power produced by the giant generators of Coulee Dam drives the pumps that lift 720,000 gallons of water per minute from the lake behind the dam and dump them into Banks Lake, from whence they are distributed to over a million acres of otherwise arid land.

Formed by the dammed up Grand Coulee, the twenty-seven-mile-long Banks Lake has a storage capacity of 1,275,000 acre-feet of water. For the first time, irrigation of the Columbia Basin was being attempted on a scale that made available sufficient quantities of water and a distribution system flexible enough to apply it. Certainly there were many problems to be overcome, some of them highly formidable, but in the heady atmosphere of a project in which accomplishing the difficult was routine and the impossible only slightly less so, that just made things more interesting.

Into the desert like an invading army rolled a massive array of earth-moving machinery. Huge tractors linked together with hundreds of yards of inch-thick steel cables uprooted sagebrush and even deeply imbedded rocks, while behind them earth-grading machines that smoothed hillocks and hollows left behind a flat, smooth surface well adapted to row-irrigation. Lumbering machines that dug a forty-foot-wide ditch and left a concrete-lined canal behind them inched along the designated boundary lines, while an army of smaller machines excavated the side feeder canals that would bring the life-giving water to all parts of the project. It was land shaping on a monumental scale and even today, over thirty years after the first irrigation water was delivered to the Basin, the work goes on; the Basin Project is a living entity whose needs are met as they become known, and it will still be many years before the entire massive complex is completed.

Technical innovations that have arrived since the beginning of the project have forced some changes in the original planning. The lands were initially classified according to soil types and the irrigation method to which they were best adapted: row-irrigation for the flat lands, portable sprinklers for the others. A large area of coarse black sands was originally bypassed, since no method then available was suitable for this type of soil. Then, in the mid 1960s, the center pivot system arrived and these previously unusable sections of "wasteland" became highly prized, extremely productive units. The only sections of the basin that are not today under active development are those that are being left in their pristine state to shelter wildlife, and even these are benefited by the rising water table that almost always improves the environment.

The first phase of the Columbia Basin Project has now been implemented, and work has started on the second Bacon Siphon, which will bring the second half-million-acre block of land under irrigation. Already, over five hundred thousand acres of formerly arid land have become some of the most highly productive farmland in the entire nation. Where the eye formerly roamed over an unlimited expanse of dusty sagebrush, it is now greeted by endless rows of green, growing plants and neat, well-planted farm buildings. Over 80,000 people now inhabit an area that formerly held only a handful, new towns have been born, and old towns, tremendously revitalized and enlarged, have become booming, bustling mercantile centers catering to the needs of a vital and burgeoning economy. Sugar beets, potatoes, alfalfa, hay, grapes, carrots: the list contains just about anything that can be grown in America north of the tropics. And since these products must be processed and marketed, the newly revitalized towns are the centers for potato processing plants, seed treating and packaging firms, canneries, dairies, even a multimillion-dollar sugar refinery. Service institutions catering to the needs of a young, growing, well-educated, and free-spending populace have risen up and prospered. Gone are the sleepy little towns where the main social event of the day was the arrival of the daily mail train. Now the towns of the Columbia River basin have all the vitality—and the growing pains—of frontier towns, which in effect they are, for the basin is a new frontier in human achievement and its people are indeed pioneers, opening up a new land and making it blossom with the fruits of their labors.

There is an air of electricity, of hard work and seized opportunity, in these new basin

A combine marches across a waving field of wheat near Walla Walla, Washington. Per acre yield in this area is one of the highest in the world.

Near Boardman, Oregon, record crops of beautiful potatoes are harvested from lands that only a few years ago were going begging at $5 per acre.

Summer Falls, near Ephrata, results from irrigation water cascading over a forty-foot cliff.

Near Moses Lake, Washington, the barren sand dunes are carpeted with desert flowers under the influence of spring rains and a warm desert sun.

towns that makes life in them anything but dull. The Basin has already produced its first millionaires and more will inevitably follow as the land reaches toward the potential which is its rightful due. Moses Lake has tripled in size since the Project started. Othello and Ephrata went from being sleepy little desert towns to busy, bustling mercantile centers. Quincy grew from a wide spot in the road to a modern, rapidly growing town that every year exceeds the expectations of even its own avid boosters. The day is past when basin towns exported their youth to more promising centers: the promised land is here and most of the young people, realizing the potential of what their parents started, are staying to reap the fruits of their hard labor.

The original unit of land in the Project was 160 acres, later increased to 320 acres for a man and wife. Many of the original units are now over twenty years old and are well-established, neat, small farms affording a good living for their occupants. Some farmers have found it to their advantage to pool their acreage and resources for greater efficiency, and these agribusinesses have become an integral part of the Basin's economy. With the high cost of today's farming, this practice will probably become more and more prevalent, since many crops are more efficiently farmed in large blocks which make large — and costly — farm machinery economically feasible.

When the first drawings for the largely federally owned land were made, preference was given to veterans who could show financial responsibility and could pass the strict criteria established for ultimate ownership. As a result, a very high class of better then average educated, highly motivated men and women became the pioneers in the Project. Their children, raised in the Basin and imbued with their parents' ideals of optimism and hard work, show every sign of carrying on the work. The future of the Project is as bright as the green of its luxuriantly growing crops.

While the main emphasis of irrigation centers in the Columbia Basin, it is not the only region that benefits from the bounty of the River. Near Burbank, at the confluence of the Snake and the Columbia, one of the world's largest contiguous vineyards spreads its several thousands of acres, some of its blocks planted to fine varietals that are already establishing an enviable reputation in the wine world.

Nearby, huge central pivot irrigation systems, each one irrigating 146 acres, slowly rotate around a fixed center point, from whence water is dispersed along a long tubular arm supported by electrically driven wheels which travel the same track over and over again and feed water to soils which could not be economically irrigated by any other current method. Fertilizers and trace elements are fed into the water before application, so that even coarse sand and gravel produce bumper crops. Every year, the organic detritus of the previous year's crop is plowed into the sandy soil so that in a few years humus has been added to a soil previously noticeably lacking in this vital ingredient. Thus, soils that only a few years ago were considered worthless — some of them went begging at five dollars an acre — are now becoming first-quality farm lands. Everywhere, in a long strip from Burbank to Boardman, the green circles of corn, wheat, alfalfa, hay, potatoes, or sugar beets thrive on water pumped from the Snake or Columbia, by pumps powered by Columbia River system energy. If ever an example were needed of how a river brings life to an otherwise arid region, one could cite the Nile — or the Columbia.

Near Boardman, Oregon, one of the rapidly growing towns on the banks of the Columbia, a group of metal framed buildings houses new food-processing facilities, a natural offshoot of the new agricultural wealth pouring from the thousands of acres of newly developed farmland along the Columbia. Only a few years ago, if a jackrabbit wanted to cross this country, he'd have had to figuratively pack a canteen, because if ever there was a blighted sun-blasted desert, this was it. Nowadays that well-fed jackrabbit would be better off wearing a raincoat, for the modern day farmer can command "rain" by pressing a button or, more usually, by letting a computer programmed to deliver the optimum amount of moisture at the proper time switch on the water as needed. From the air, as far as the eye can see, on both sides of the River, are hundreds of green circles exuberantly growing the foodstuffs America — and the world — needs, on land that only ten years ago grew only sagebrush and an occasional sunburned cactus.

Developing this land on a large scale takes massive amounts of capital, so it is no surprise that this is largely the domain of the large agribusinesses. A battery of twelve- to sixty-three-hundred-horsepower pumps, several miles of twenty-four-inch welded steel pipe, and dozens or even hundreds of expensive center pivot irrigation systems, plus the manpower needed to maintain an establishment of this size predicate the investment of several million dollars, a sum far beyond the reach of the average small farmer. As in the Columbia Basin, a partial answer to this problem has been achieved by several small farmers pooling their holdings and capital into one large business. Several large blocks of land are farmed by conglomerates; near Boardman, one of the prime developers of 60,000 acres of desert land has been the Boeing Company. In the initial stages of their farming operation, when they were faced with the problem of holding in place the sand uncovered by their tractors as the sagebrush was ripped out, the Boeing people resorted to have bargeloads of organic garbage towed upstream from Portland to be mixed into the sandy soil, so that the ubiquitous Columbia River winds would not blow away their farm before they had a chance to till it. Now, after several seasons of plowing in "green fertilizer" cover crops, the land is sufficiently stabilized that the garbage is no longer needed. It certainly was an intriguing form of recycling while it lasted.

The effects of irrigation on the economy of the lands contiguous to the Columbia and in the Columbia Basin are perhaps not really yet appreciated by most of the people of the region, even those living close to the irrigated lands. It is pretty much taken for granted, like sunshine, spring rain, or good health and probably would be fully appreciated only if it were to be suddenly taken away. But the process whereby worthless land is transformed into a garden, the desert made to bear fruit on command, and the whole economy of a region immeasurably enriched smacks of a major miracle. It could be done only because the Columbia provides water for irrigation as well as cheap, ample power to pump that water. The immediate tangible results of this transformation are astounding enough, but the side benefits that accrue when a formerly arid region is turned into a well-watered one also cannot be ignored.

All through the Columbia Basin, new lakes that are a direct result of the irrigation project are providing sportsmen and vacationers with new playgrounds and supporting an actively proliferating wildlife where practically none previously existed. A sparsely populated, unproductive desert has been transformed into a rich, productive, well-populated region teeming with new life.

A miracle has taken place in the desert.

The River and the Atom

THE PART PLAYED BY THE Columbia River as a prime producer of energy that made possible the production miracles of World War II has already been noted and is generally well known. Not so well known is the decisive part the River played in bringing the war to a victorious conclusion, for this role was shrouded in mystery and constitutes one of the best kept secrets of those troubled times. Yet, the effects of the drama begun on the banks of the Columbia River changed history and forever altered the course of human events, for the Atomic Age can trace a good part of its birth back to the events that began here in January 1943.

When Enrico Fermi and his band of dedicated experimenters first activated a small atomic pile under the grandstand of the University of Chicago in 1942, they proved on a practical basis that not only was the theorem first advanced by Albert Einstein in 1906 sound, but that utilizing the awesome power locked up in the atom was feasible. To a nation then struggling in the throes of a titanic war, the promise

A few miles north of Richland, Washington, the Fast Flux Test Reactor tests nuclear plant components under actual operating conditions.

of a new weapon of fantastic power was irresistible, especially since the the best available intelligence reports repeatedly stressed that the enemy was devoting unusually large amounts of energy and scientific talent toward the attainment of that same end.

President Franklin Delano Roosevelt and the War Council, after consulting with Dr. Einstein and others active in atomic research, decided to go ahead with a massive project aimed at obtaining a nuclear weapon ahead of the Axis powers. The result was the Manhattan Project, one of the most daring and successful engineering projects ever undertaken by man. And the Columbia River was an integral part of it.

Even in a country as large and diversified as the United States, there were not too many sites available for an engineering complex of the magnitude and peculiar requirements of the Manhattan Project. Since its purpose was the building of chemical plants and reactors that would make fuel for a successful atomic weapon, security was of the utmost importance. The project should be situated in a sparsely settled and geographically stable area, and it should have ample supplies of cold, clean water and electrical energy.

In the desert near the small town (population 250) of Richland, Washington, a 640-square-mile section of desert on the banks of the coldest, cleanest large river in the United States and with the newly abundant electrical energy of Grand Coulee Dam only 100 miles away was designated as the Hanford Engineering Works and was given top priority for men and materiel.

The building of Hanford is the stuff of which legends are spun. In a few months, a theretofore barren and unpopulated section of desert had a population of 51,000 men and women working around the clock, housed in long, newly erected barracks and fed in mammoth mess halls that never closed. In the desert, millions of cubic yards of concrete were poured by workmen working from blueprints newly supplied each day and who didn't have the faintest idea of what they were building. Conjectures ran all the way from the ridiculous to some pretty close guesses that a highly sophicticated chemical product was meant to be produced there. Security was practically airtight, and in the work force, plainclothes FBI agents were liberally mixed in with the average

working man. No one, not even the highest ranking official, was exempt from the rigorous search programs instituted at each closely guarded gate. Guards with leashed dogs patrolled the desert perimeter, light planes patrolled every back road, and antiaircraft guns studded the borders of the installation. Those gunners had orders to shoot down any unauthorized aircraft that flew over the area—and they did, as several aberrant crews from the nearby bomber training stations at Pasco, Walla Walla, and Pendleton discovered to their consternation.

The complex itself consisted of three reactors and the chemical processing plants that separated the basic uranium from the plutonium resulting from the atomic reaction. These installations were linked by miles of hard-topped roads and railroad sidings whose steel fingers probed every part of the several hundred square miles behind the "Barrier," as the limiting perimeter was called. Because the wartime reactors depended on large quantities of cold, clear coolant water from the Columbia, the reactors were built close to the river, while the separation facilities were farther inland.

The wartime reactors were basically huge cubes of honeycombed graphite in which slugs of metallic uranium encased in long steel tubes could be placed. When enough of this radioactive metal (a "critical mass") was brought into juxtaposition, nuclear fission spontaneously began. To control this reaction, control rods of a substance (usually boron or cadmium) which absorbed a certain percentage of the neutrons that are a product of the nuclear reaction were strategically placed in the pile and the whole huge cube was cooled by large amounts of cold Columbia River water running through miles of piping. The water emerged from the pile hot enough to require cooling in special settling ponds before it was returned to the river, but even so the Columbia below Hanford ran very slightly warmer than it did above the installation. In this present day of heightened environmental concern, this probably would have evoked anguished cries of "thermal pollution" from the more ardent environmentalists and probably resulted in a rash of lawsuits all aimed at curbing a situation that in their eyes would have irretrievably ruined the whole downriver Columbia River system. Fortunately for the war effort, the term "thermal pollution" was still practically unknown and the slightly warmer

Columbia unconcernedly wended its way to the sea, with absolutely no deleterious effects from the warmer water introduced into it at Hanford. Subject to today's stringent ecological standards and sometimes hysterical interpretation, the whole project probably would have been closed down and the program that had a decisive role in ending the war aborted.

Once the slugs of uranium had been irradiated, they were removed from the reactor and moved to the chemical separation plants, where their small content of plutonium was chemically extracted. The rest of the uranium 235, recast into slugs, was run through the reactor again. The processes by which the irradiated uranium was separated from the plutonium were (and still are) some of the most delicate and complicated chemical operations known to man, requiring tremendously complicated and sophisticated chemical engineering and facilities. Working behind heavy concrete walls, peering through up to thirty inches of heavy high-lead-content glass, and using remotely controlled robot arms to handle dangerously radioactive materials was bad enough, but the knowledge that they were pioneering new paths of scientific achievement daily must have been a sobering thought for the men and women who were the first workers in the new atomic plants. There was no precedent to follow: they were writing the book on the treatment of atomic materials as they went along, because each step in the process was a scientific first. It is a tribute to the care and dedication of the people who worked on those first plants that, without a serious or even minor accident, they separated enough plutonium to make the Nagasaki bomb that ended the war. What makes it all the more wonderful is that they didn't even know what they were making!

The scientists who wrote the specifications for those atomic plants were likewise faced with a dilemma. They knew an atomic bomb was theoretically feasible. But would it really work and, if it did, would the reaction be controllable? The answer came on that April morning at Alamogordo when the predawn darkness of the desert was shattered by an incandescent fireball of such gigantic proportions that even the men who had created it were stunned by its immensity. It worked, all right, and the world, for good or evil, was ushered into the Atomic Age.

For all the thousands of people who were employed at Richland and Hanford, the secret was remarkably well kept. Until two incandescent fireballs over Hiroshima and Nagasaki dramatically ushered in the era of atomic warfare, most people had never heard of an atomic bomb, let alone the fact that the United States had taken only twenty-seven months to perfect the tremendously complicated technology necessary for its production. Even to the thousands of workers who had built the vast plants at Hanford and Oak Ridge, the news of Hiroshima came as a stunning surprise. Captured enemy intelligence documents indicate that while the massive construction projects going on at these sites were well known to the enemy, their purpose was as much a secret to them as it was to the men and women who were building the installations.

The chemical plants and the reactors in which the complex nuclear reactions took place are still at Hanford. The reactors, with the exemption of the N-Reactor, which produces not only plutonium but also from its byproduct steam as much electrical energy as a large

Prototype core-emplacement machine for the Fast Flux Test Reactor, Hanford Atomic Reservation.

hydroelectric dam, are still in existence but deactivated. The "B" Reactor, which produced the first plutonium used in a nuclear weapon, has been designated a National Engineering Monument but is deserted and dark, while other wartime reactors are waiting to be torn down.

It is an eerie feeling, on seeing these huge blocks of honeycombed graphite with their myriad arrays of hoses and pipes, to realize that one of the greatest steps in man's scientific evolution took place in these buildings. Whether it was a forward or backward step may be questioned by some, but the fact remains that in these places the mysteries of matter were unraveled, the ancient dreams of the alchemists, the transmutation of metals, were finally realized, and the sum total of human knowledge greatly increased. Whether the knowledge gained here is used for good or evil is not the question: that is controlled by an entirely different set of circumstances; but strictly as an engineering project, the accomplishments of the men and women, laymen and scientists alike, who built the Hanford Engineering Works will always stand as a masterpiece of achievement in the annals of human progress.

The building days at Hanford are remembered by many who still work there. They were never easy: conditions were primitive, privacy was a very scarce commodity, and living under conditions of the very strictest security was something pretty onerous. The sandy soil around the newly erected prefabs at Richland blew into the houses at every breeze, and neat housekeeping became an impossible task. Many of the new employees couldn't take the primitive living conditions, and turnover was very high, but somehow the monumental construction job was done. Slowly a viable city began to emerge from the sagebrush and sand dunes.

Many people thought that the conclusion of the war would bring an end to Richland and the Hanford Works. Instead, it brought a new burst of activity. The original project had been built by the DuPont Corporation under the direction of the U.S. Army Corps of Engineers, but in 1947 a new phase of construction began under the aegis of the newly formed Atomic Energy Commission (AEC), which turned over the direction of the plant to the General Electric Company on January 1.

In a period when America was faced with

the problem of redesigning its whole strategic arsenal to fit the nuclear concept, the original three reactors at Hanford, practically worn out by their strenuous wartime usage, were redesigned for new and greater efficiency. Five new reactors were installed. This was the period of the Cold War and it produced a burst of building activity which, if it were not as frantic as that of the war years, was at least as extensive. A whole new city grew up at North Richland to house the thousands of construction workers involved in building the new reactors behind the Barrier, and Richland doubled in population. The adjacent cities of Pasco and Kennewick, which had served to a great extent as bedroom communities, also grew considerably, and the ancillary services required by the new population gave these communities the impetus they needed to start them on their march to greatness. The Tri-Cities began their amazing growth, becoming one of the most rapidly developing areas of the Northwest. A new business district, ten blocks north of Richland's old city center, was built and remains as the mercantile center of the present city. Housing was still critical and completely controlled by the AEC. It wasn't till 1957 that Richland ceased to be a company town and private home ownership became possible.

There are still many signs of wartime construction in present-day Richland. Scores of houses, even though altered and landscaped, evince the "barracks modern" type of architecture ground out by a construction force more intent on achieving production than variety. But along with the old construction, a definitely new look has come to Richland. With the advent of private ownership, handsome new homes especially adapted to the sun-filled desert style of living have been built. Swimming pools and private tennis courts are common, and the life style definitely reflects the tastes of an urbane, well-educated, and affluent society. Richland is well on its way to becoming a handsome city even if an occasional vacant lot still sports a crest of sagebrush and wind blown sand, as though it were reminding the present occupants that the desert is near and, without constant attention, would soon reclaim its own.

The really big changes in the Atomic City came in 1964, when President Lyndon B. Johnson announced the cutback in plutonium production that would result in the shutdown of all but the newest reactor. Many thought it would be the end of Hanford and its appendage city, Richland. Actually, it signaled the beginning of Hanford's most productive phase.

The emphasis shifted away from the production of plutonium for weapons and toward the usage of atomic power and products for peaceful purposes. Research and development companies moved in, and in a few years the ground lost in the 1964 cutbacks had been regained and even exceeded. The pool of brainpower and skilled craftsmanship available at Richland was such that industry moved to it, rather than vice versa, because most of the people had become so enamored of their life style by the banks of the Columbia that they simply would not willingly move away.

At present, by far the greater part of the activity at Hanford is slanted toward research and the peaceful applications of nuclear energy. The disposal of nuclear wastes which are an inevitable by-product of the atomic process also rates a very high priority, and Hanford has become a disposal site where much of the low-radiation-level material produced by the industry is safely stored. The peculiar geology of the Hanford area, which largely dictated the choice of this site in the first place, makes this feasible as well as making it a prime candidate for the permanent disposal of long-lived, high-energy radioactive materials. Opponents of this system decry it. What they don't realize is that the bulk of the material deposited here emits considerably less radiation than the luminescent watches many of them routinely wear every day.

In the late 1970s and early 1980s, a definite change occurred in the projections for energy needed in the Pacific Northwest. Made acutely aware of its energy vulnerability by the Arab oil embargo of 1973, America embarked on a long overdue energy conservation program that dramatically cut its use of all types of energy, including electrical. While the demand for energy will unquestionably grow in years to come, the previous projections which showed a dramatic need for more energy in the decades ahead have been revamped.

This new conservation, coupled with the decreased usage of energy by industries hard hit by the recession of the early eighties, has slowed the demand for new energy-producing plants, both hydroelectric and nuclear. The Tri-Cities area has been hit, and hit hard, by this recession. Construction activity has slowed, and in this field unemployment is high. Never-

theless, it is significant that the majority of the workers stay in the area if it is at all possible. The way of life to which they have become accustomed is much too pleasant to be permanently abandoned, even if temporary conditions dictate that some adjustments must be made in their life style. There is always tomorrow, and nowhere do the promises of a better tomorrow glow more brightly than on the banks of the Columbia.

Hanford is the site of the large Washington Public Power Supply System (WPPSS) installations which have been very much in the news for some time and probably will continue to be for some years. Started at a time when projections for power needs all indicated that at least five new nuclear plants would be needed, they were plagued from their inception by cost overruns, mostly caused by constant design changes. Strangled in red tape regulations and sometimes irresponsible ecological controls, they have become a source of controversy, so much so that in 1982 two of the three plants being built at Hanford were mothballed and will not be completed until the demand for energy makes them economically feasible. The third, 90 percent completed, went on line in 1984 and provides as much electrical energy as a large hydroelectric dam.

The WPPSS plants are being built on the Hanford Reservation on land leased from the Department of Energy (DOE) and will firmly establish the region as the world's center of nuclear energy . . . unless the opponents of all nuclear energy prevail. It is sad to think that the lead in nuclear power should have passed from the United States, where it was born, to France and the Soviet Union. There, plants are built to much less stringent safety regulations, and Soviet opponents to their erection, if they surface at all, are quickly and usefully employed mining gold at Kolyma, where the numbing cold quickly cools their ardor.

While the recession of the 1980s and the conservation efforts that have so drastically cut the use of electrical energy have revamped the projections for new power usage, the curve for energy demand, for new power, continues to rise and will intersect the curve for ultimate hydroelectric production on the River in the late 1980s. Those plants will almost certainly be built, and the sooner they are completed, the less they will cost.

The WPPSS reactors are all of similar construction, a system tested in the present N-Reactor and found to be very reliable. Each installation will consist of a central reactor core in which superheated water in a closed loop will transfer heat to a secondary loop. From there, it will be flashed into steam and fed under high pressure to four large turbines, each designed to operate at successively lower pressures. These turbines will spin a large 1,250-megawatt generator at 1,800 revolutions per minute and produce as much electrical energy as a large Columbia River dam. Marvels of complexity and sophisticated engineering, these installations, with their myriad safety control features and cooling towers, will each cost many millions of dollars but will provide the energy needed in a world where hydroelectric potential has been reached, fossil fuel prices and restrictions have become prohibitive, and solar power is a dream yet to be realized.

The WPPSS organization has achieved a rather dubious distinction. Caught in a stran-

Loading face of the N-Reactor, which produces both steam for power generation and plutonium for nuclear weapons.

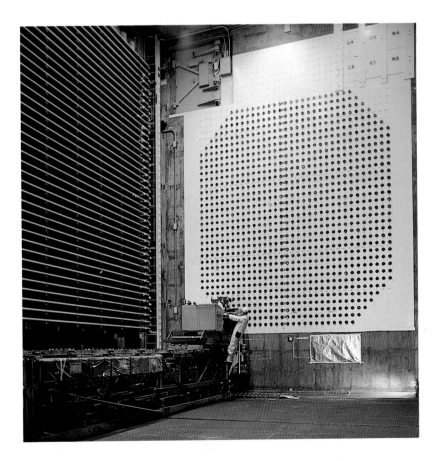

gling web of cost overruns, design changes, federal regulations, and labor troubles, the WPPSS in January 1984 formally defaulted on its bonds, thus creating the largest bond default in United States history. The consequent litigation and controversy have had much to do with undermining public and investment confidence in nuclear energy and can only be viewed as a backward step in the development of nuclear power in the United States

In 1965 a change was made in the method of operating the Hanford Engineering Works. Various segments of the operations were entrusted to private contractors, who each pledged to bring new, ancillary jobs to the area. The idea was to keep Richland from becoming a one-employer town with all the problems such a situation inevitably brings. The diversification, last implemented in 1967, has been highly successful and continues to the present day.

The overall operation of the Hanford Works was entrusted to the Energy Research and Development Administration (ERDA), which took over from the old Atomic Energy Commission, which was succeeded by the present Department of Energy (DOE). As its title suggests, the present agency is concerned with energy in any form, although at Hanford the emphasis is predictably nuclear.

Today, there are four major contractors at Hanford. One of these, the Energy Systems Group of Rockwell International, is entrusted with the major problem of solidifying and managing the millions of gallons of liquid atomic wastes that had accumulated during the thirty-five years or so that Hanford has been in operation. New, double-wall tanks are being installed and the old liquids are boiled down to a still highly radioactive, slushy "salt cake" concentrate. High-heat-producing isotopes such as cesium 135 and strontium 90 are separated, sealed in strong stainless steel containers, and stored in a water-filled thirteen-foot vault where their unearthly blue glow (due to the Cherenkov effect) is a constant reminder of the heat and radioactivity they will emit for years. The less radioactive salts can be converted to insoluble glass that is easily stored or buried. Medicine, science, the space program, and industry are constantly finding new uses for the other isotopes so that yesterday's nuisance is rapidly becoming today's chemical frontier, a situation analogous to that of the coal tar which for so many years was a messy, unwelcome by-product of the coal-gas industry until scientists discovered that it could be converted into dyes, pharmaceuticals, and even perfumes. Rockwell also has charge of chemical processing and support service for the entire site.

The chief research facility at Hanford is that of the Battelle Memorial Institute, which is housed in a handsome, low, pebbled-exterior concrete laboratory and office that is a marvel of functional and aesthetic efficiency. One of the nation's leading and most complete research facilities, Battelle is interested in all aspects of producing energy, whether from the atom, the earth, or the sky. It also administers the 120-square-mile Arid Lands Ecology Project, where all aspects of life in the desert are documented and studied. Atop Rattlesnake Mountain, Battelle houses a large reflecting telescope manned by very competent young scientists eager to delve into the mysteries of space. The main laboratory houses the latest, most advanced research equipment and a host of razor-sharp researchers to whom the unknown is a fascinating frontier waiting to be explored.

United Nuclear Industries operates the only producing reactor at Hanford and serves as a custodian for four others which are kept on a standby basis. The N-Reactor that produces the plutonium needed to keep America's nuclear arsenal up to date also produces steam which is sold to the adjacent WPPSS electrical generating plant. There, steam produced by the heat of the atomic fission process runs two massive turbines, producing as much electrical energy as a large hydroelectric plant. The many advantages of nuclear power were most evident during the 1977 drought, when water supplies even in the usually reliable Columbia were so curtailed that the energy output of the WPPSS plant became essential and spelled the big difference between normal business operations in the Northwest and a severe brownout. Taking advantage of the nuclear know-how situated in and around Richland, United Nuclear also operates a full fabrication system that employs many skilled operators and has a worldwide clientele.

Westinghouse Hanford Company is in charge of the Hanford Engineering Development Laboratory (HEDL) for the DOE. The lab's main occupation at Hanford is the development of an experimental breeder reactor where the various components needed for the new type of energy can be tested. To implement this research, HEDL has built the world's largest experimental breeder reactor seven miles north of Richland—and it is something one has to see to really believe.

Strange as it may sound, the breeder produces more usable nuclear fuel than it consumes. It does this by having its core, where the fission reaction takes place, surrounded by uranium 238, a fertile material which will react with or absorb neutrons and result in a new fissionable material, plutonium 239. The new material, placed in a different reactor, can produce more neutrons via the fission process, breed more plutonium, and thus make the operation self-perpetuating. Since fertile material is relatively abundant, the breeder reactor can produce heat and electricity long past the period in which the demand for electrical energy has exceeded the supply generated by running water. But before the breeder can realize its potential, many technical questions must be answered, and the Fast Flux Test Facility (FFTF) at the site is designed to provide those answers.

The FFTF produces no electricity, and the enormous heat it generates is vented into the desert air via very large, blocky heat exchangers. Within its commodious conical containment dome is crammed some of the most ingenious and technologically sophisticated equipment ever devised by man. Massive cranes can lift component parts of the breeder itself, or parts for future breeders, which will be placed in the large testing chamber where they will be subjected to the toughest conditions they could possibly undergo in actual use. Here the technology of heat transfer by liquid sodium, conduct of metals under conditions of intensive radiation, and the suitability of any component can be evaluated under actual working conditions before it is put to work in an operating reactor. The FFTF is a marvel of imaginative engineering and precision workmanship, a useful probe into the problems that must and will be solved before the breeder reactor, with all its advantages, can take its place in the energy field of the future.

The FFTF is the largest reactor in the world devoted solely to research and certainly the most expensive. Sophisticated engineering and construction never did come cheaply, and this structure is about as intricate and sophisticated as they come, as a beautifully detailed model in the nearby visitor's center will demonstrate. This exhibit can be reached by a highway north from Richland and has already deservedly become an outstanding tourist attraction.

THERE ARE REAL PROBLEMS attendant to the production of electricity by atomic fission, some very real and some mostly imaginary. The imaginary problems, unfortunately, can present every bit as many obstacles as the valid problems, because a generation of people brought up on atomic knowledge gleaned from comic strips and sensational TV programs in which atomic energy is invariably cast as the villain often cannot differentiate between the valid and invalid. It is really a pity that the first application of atomic power smashed a city and thus became in the minds of many people a symbol of evil incarnate. The fact that the atomic bombs that ended World War II took many lives is vividly remembered, etched in the minds of people all over the world in memories as bright as the fireballs that doomed Hiroshima and Nagasaki.

Many of the people who live in Richland and who have lived in the shadow of nine of the world's largest reactors for thirty-five years, view with bemused amazement the outside world's fear of atomic energy. They certainly do not denigrate the power of the atom: no one holds it in greater respect, because no one understands it better. They also don't fear it, because they recognize that it is a force subject to physical laws and, when treated with the respect it demands, a useful and compliant servant. That it can be, like fire, a very bad master is also recognized, and so you see around Hanford a healthy respect for the atom, mixed with a certain amount of condescending contempt for the mentality of people whose knowledge of atomic energy has been gleaned largely from watching "The Incredible Hulk" and doomsday type TV specials in which atomic energy makes a handy if not completely understood villain. A research physicist at Hanford who probably knows as much about atomic energy as anyone once summed it up for me in words that for their sheer simplicity are hard to beat.

"I've lived here," he said, "within a few miles of these reactors ever since they went critical in 1943. I've married, raised four beautiful children, and am now enjoying twelve grandchildren, all born here and healthy as can be. Do

you think I'd risk all that if I thought there were any foundation at all to the fears that so many people have about atomic energy?"

The truth is that there have been only three accidental deaths in the nuclear energy field in the United States since its inception and those were way back in the fifties, at the Arco Research Center in Idaho. No other industry can even come close to equaling this safety record. The people of the Tri-Cities, who from long and safe association with the atom have no inordinate fear of it, point to this safety record with pride and so create a political climate that attracts nuclear-related industry to the area.

Scientists at Hanford readily agree that nuclear power is only an interim step toward the achievement of the ultimate source of energy, solar power. Yet, they consider it an essential step, just as the steam engine was the principal source of motile industrial power in the nineteenth century before the introduction of the internal combustion engine and electric motor. This step, they feel, must be taken if we are to have a workable source of energy before man learns to utilize the fantastic energy potential in sunlight, which every day showers on the face of the earth more energy than all mankind uses in a year.

The River also had a part in another atomic development, one not as extensive as Hanford but which seems to get a disportionately large share of publicity. Travelers on Interstate 5 near Kalama see, looming on the opposite side of the Columbia, a 500-foot-high cooling tower. Aircraft-warning strobe lights flash night and day from its perimeter, and on cool days a flowing plume of steam streams from its top. Immaculately groomed grounds and reflecting lagoons mirror a domed containment vessel and beautifully landscaped buildings where two very large generators hum night and day with steam produced by Oregon's only atomic reactor.

This is the Portland General Electric atomic installation at Rainier, a nuclear-powered electrical generating station that has produced both large quantities of electricity and controversy.

Again, the cooling capacity of the Columbia was the main reason for building this installation on the banks of the River. Water from the river is used to cool and moderate the atomic pile and is brought back to the normal temperature of the river in the cooling tower before being returned to the stream. Large quantities of river water cascade from the interior of the giant hollow shell and mingle with the water from the secondary heat transfer loop of the pile.

Some opponents of nuclear power view with alarm the recycling of this water that has helped cool the elemental heat of the atom, even if only secondarily, thinking the river will certainly be polluted with long-lasting radioactivity. Actually, water is one of the best moderators of an atomic reaction and, if absolutely pure, does not become radioactive, although a very small part of the total amount will be decomposed into elemental hydrogen and oxygen. Of course, salts dissolved in water, especially from a radioactive substance, would make the solution radioactive, but none of the water that is returned to the river is ever allowed to contact a radioactive salt. It will issue from the pile thermally hot, but without a trace of radioactivity. The gases resulting from atomic disintegration of water do have some short-lived radioactivity, but these are burned to form water again, which is either returned to the primary closed loop or allowed to decay till no discernible radioactivity remains.

The Rainier plant, situated relatively near a large city, has been a favorite target of those adamantly opposed to nuclear power. There is even an active group whose avowed purpose is to permanently close down the one-billion-dollar-plus facility as unsafe. The fact that the Rainier plant is a well-designed, beautifully maintained facility and that atomic plants are the most closely monitored source of energy in existence seems to make no difference. The fact that the output of the plant is desperately needed and would be impossible to replace is conveniently overlooked or disregarded. During the 1977 drought, when hydroelectrically generated energy was in short supply, the Rainier plant and the other atomic installation at Hanford kept the energy load at a workable level and demonstrated dramatically the practicality of this space-age method of electrical generation.

Unlike the River, which has a definite limit to its generating capacity, atomic energy is limited only by the availability of suitable sites and atomic fuel. Research aimed at using thorium rather than uranium for the fissionable material in the new generation of breeder reactors is well under way and, when it has worked out the problems attendant to the new material, will remove the biggest stumbling block that keeps the breeder reactor from being readily accepted, at least by the vast majority of the scientific world.

Conventional breeders, using uranium as a fuel, convert that uranium to plutonium. Plutonium 239 can fuel other reactors, but given sufficient refining and treatment, it also is the principal ingredient of atomic weaponry. There is a fear, and unfortunately a very justifiable one, that plutonium intended for a reactor could be surreptitiously diverted into an atomic weapon which could be used by terrorist groups or an unprincipled nation for atomic blackmail. This has been the theme of countless novels and TV shows and is a scenario readily believed by a general public that has no idea of the complexity of the chemical process that produces weapons-grade plutonium.

At present, the United States has a virtual monopoly on the production of fuel rods, at least for American-made reactors, and insists that the spent rods be returned to this country for treatment. However, the technology of atomic fuels is well understood, well within the reach of any technologically advanced nation or organization, and it is only a matter or time until some group or nation follows India's example and produces an atomic weapon using plutonium extracted from fuel rods irradiated in a commercial reactor. The danger in atomic proliferation is obvious and constitutes the single largest obstacle to the general usage of this new form of energy.

In spite of the problems, atomic energy is so convenient, offers such a solution to the world's energy demands, and is such a concentrated source of power that it will inevitably be used more and more by a society every day more technologically oriented. And the advance will more than likely be spearheaded in those places that originally gave birth to the atomic industry.

High on that list will be the city on the banks of the Columbia that the atom built. The future of Hanford is already blueprinted. More and more, it will become an atomic research and manufacturing center where the full potential of the atom will be studied, analyzed, and put to work. As such, it can be truthfully said that this is one of the most important places in the United States and the world.

The drama begun on the banks of the Columbia River is only in its first act.

Highway to the Sea

FOR UNTOLD CENTURIES BEFORE the white man came to the Pacific Northwest, the native tribes were using, as a natural gift from the gods, the convenient highway to the sea that is the Columbia River. From far inland and from its principal tributary, the Snake, dugout canoes regularly made the sometimes perilous journey down the Great River, bringing the buffalo hides, furs, stone arrowheads, and basketwork of the interior to the coast, where they were bartered for dried fish, beadwork, furs, and carved wooden utensils. It may have been primitive by modern standards, but a brisk trade existed on the Columbia and did much to bring together tribes that would have otherwise had contact with each other only in warfare.

Then, as now, the Columbia was the natural artery of commerce for the people of the Northwest, for the drainage area of the vast river found, in the network of streams leading to the Great River, the only convenient method of transportation in a roadless land. The Columbia is the only natural water-level opening to the coast in a string of mountains stretching for

The Middle Columbia sees a steady string of tugs and barges transporting bulk cargo to and from the Inland Empire.

over seven hundred miles and so was the natural funnel for the commerce that would inevitably occur when one region needed the products of another and had the means of importing them. True, it was not always a smooth, level highway, for the river was prone to sudden storms and studded with hidden perils, from barely submerged rocks in boiling rapids to rapacious tribes eager to exact tribute from anyone using the river at their door.

The Indians traveled the River in dugout canoes, some of them, especially those of the coastal tribes, of great length and fine workmanship. Usually made of hollowed out cedar, these canoes were stable enough to weather the storms and rapids of the Columbia and brave the murderous Bar which challenged the seamanship of even the finest white sailors. Lewis and Clark describe these native canoeists as "the finest in the world" and marvel at length at the seeming ease with which they negotiated the perilous rapids of the swift coastal streams.

Lewis and Clark had only a limited acquaintance with the voyageurs, or they might have qualified their statements about the Indian canoeists. Renowned in song and story as the most intrepid boatmen the American continent has ever produced, these laughing daredevils would take their heavily laden, high-prowed, double-ended boats anywhere there was enough water to float them, easily negotiating twisting, rock-studded rapids with the unerring skill born of a lifetime of practice. Their Gallic exuberance, however, was mixed with a certain amount of Indian pragmatism. To the uninitiated, it seemed that they were taking foolish chances, whereas in practical fact, whenever they decided to shoot a seemingly impossible rapids rather than portage their heavy bateaux, it was only because they had shrewdly assessed their chances of making it safely through the maelstrom and decided that their skill and daring gave them the edge necessary for triumph over seemingly impossible odds. The voyageurs were the lifeblood of early Northwest trade by the white man, and their main artery was the Columbia.

From Columbia Lake at its source to its mouth at Astoria, the Columbia is almost totally navigable. The upper end had many rapids, but only one of these, Death Rapids, was regularly portaged. The others occasionally exacted their grim toll, but usually the heavy bateaux and lighter trade canoes made it through to the placid Arrow Lakes, which to the voyageur were unalloyed bliss. On these beautiful, calm waters the voyageurs' lilting songs echoed from the cliffs as the rhythmic beat of their flashing paddles carried them almost two hundred miles to their next arduous portage, Kettle Falls. Here, the heavy boats were carried around the twenty-foot falls, relations with the natives were reaffirmed, and the voyage resumed down the swift-flowing Columbia. Rock Island and Priest Rapids were "red neckerchief water," as was Umatilla Rapids, but the next big obstacle was Celilo Falls. Here the Wishram Indians, the Trojans of their day, exacted tribute from all passers and as a result were the richest and most hated Indians on the whole river. On occasion, when the waters were high and the tribute demanded even higher, some of the more daring voyageurs actually shot the twenty-foot falls and lived to boast about it; but usually it was a transfer spot where goods were transferred to the more seaworthy coastal canoes. The spine-chilling rapids of Les Dalles ("the narrow places"), where the river was constricted to a channel deeper than it was wide and ran like a mill race through a rock-studded channel, was next. This was usually shot in grim silence punctuated only by an occasional shouted command, for the power of the river at this spot is absolutely terrifying, with vortices and undercurrents that can effortlessly suck in or disgorge a twenty-foot log—or a trade canoe.

Forty miles downstream was the Cascades, a terrifying, rock-studded chute with no discernible passage, which was usually portaged. During flood periods it was sometimes negotiated—but not usually a second time by the same person. From this point, the rapids were usually negotiable till the ameliorating effects of the ocean tides began to be felt near the present location of Washougal. The rest of the run to the coast was usually pure pleasure, with the swiftly flowing river aiding the paddlers on their leisurely run to Fort Vancouver or the sea.

For forty years the bateaux and trade canoes of the voyageurs dominated trade on the Columbia. From the far-flung outposts of the Hudson's Bay Company's stations on the Arrow Lakes, the Spokane, Okanogan, and Snake, the heavily laden canoes would make an annual mass migration down the river and return laden with the trade goods and staples that would keep the inland posts functioning for another year. Oceangoing ships would tie up at Fort

Vancouver, bringing in the myriad articles that trade with the Indians required, and bringing back to England the furs that were the main export of the post. In 1835 the Company ushered in a new era of transportation on the Columbia when they sent the small steamer *Beaver* to ply the lower waters of the river, although it would be a full two decades before the "fire canoes," as the Indians called them, became the dominant mode of transportation on the river.

When Lewis and Clark came to the Northwest, they followed the natural highway to the sea which is the Columbia River. Later settlers to the Oregon Territory coming over the Blue Mountains to Marcus Whitman's mission at Wailatpu usually followed the Walla Walla River to its junction with the Columbia, where the Hudson's Bay post of Fort Walla Walla was located. There, many of them, sick and tired of the bad water, alkali dust, and unremitting toil of overland travel, elected to go the greater part of the way to the Willamette Valley by water. The prairie schooners that had carried the pioneers over a thousand miles of wilderness and desert were dismantled, loaded onto crude rafts or flatboats, and entrusted to the mercies of a pitiless river. Guided more or less by cumbersome sweeps that more often than not snapped off under the pressure of the first white water, most of these makeshift affairs actually held together under the poundings of the Umatilla Rapids, although tragedies such as that of the Applegate family at The Dalles—two members of the family were drowned in the rapids—were inevitable. The big wonder is that any of them at all survived, because these pioneers, in their ignorance, actually braved and survived rapids that even the amphibious voyageurs viewed with considerable respect.

The end of the Oregon Trail was Les Dalles, the present-day The Dalles. Here the wagons were reassembled and the rest of the journey completed, usually along the north bank of the Columbia, although after 1846 the perilous Barlow Road across the flanks of Mount Hood was the usual route.

The discovery of gold in California in 1848 had a profound effect on the economy of the Pacific Northwest. Gold fever swept the country and overnight whole communities were denuded of their menfolk in a wild stampede for the banks of the Sacramento and the fortunes that were reportedly there for the taking.

A few of the more astute settlers, shrewdly assessing the needs of the newly affluent miners, figured they could get as rich or richer by staying home and supplying the demands of the Forty-Niners. And they were right! Overnight, timber that had been piled and burned as a nuisance was worth a fortune in the gold fields of California and in the newly burgeoning city by the Golden Gate. Eggs delivered in San Francisco were sold for a dollar apiece, a bushel of apples for one hundred dollars, and bacon for up to twenty dollars a pound. Demand vastly exceeded supply, and to men for whom gold dust was an everyday, sometimes even plentiful commodity, price was no object.

In those days of casual refrigeration, it was not unusual for a shipload of produce to reach the Golden Gate in such sad state that even the food-hungry miners balked at eating it. Sailing ships, though refined to a fine art, still were at the mercy of vagrant winds, and so it was only a matter of time till the faster and more reliable steamships supplanted sail. Demand is usually met by supply, so as early as 1851 steamships began to be built in the Northwest, and a thriving new industry quickly took root.

In a few short years, steamers dominated the trade on the Columbia. Large stern wheelers, some of them nearly two hundred feet long, were transported in pieces to the Cascades and Celilo Falls, there to be reassembled and ply their own particular stretch of the river. The Cascades and Celilo Falls were never ascended, although the daring Capt. Marshall Martineau, in the true spirit of his voyageur ancestors, tried to line the steamer *D. S. Baker* over the Lower Cascades during the great flood of 1894 and almost made it. The river soon became divided into sections, each connected to the other by portage tramways. The lower section ran from Astoria to the Lower Cascades, where a portage railroad, later replaced by a canal and locks, transferred freight and passengers to the Middle River stretch, which ended at The Dalles. There, another portage railroad carried upriver freight around the treacherous falls and rapids of The Dalles and Celilo to the Upper River. On this stretch, freight and passengers could go either up the Snake to Lewiston or up the Columbia to Kettle Falls with a few anxious moments at Priest and Rock Island rapids. Wenatchee and Brewster became roaring steamboat towns, and with the advent of the Cariboo gold strike in 1862, steamboat traffic extended up the Columbia as far as Death Rapids.

As had been the case in 1849, steamboating on the Columbia got its next big boost from a gold strike. In 1860, fine placer gold was found at Orofino on the Clearwater and at Pierce, a few miles inland. Overnight, demand for passage up the Columbia soared to fantastic heights as those who had missed the California strike determined not to be left out of this one. Steamers disembarked those in a hurry at Wallula, whence they went overland to Walla Walla by a well-worn trail that quickly became a road of sorts, then by horse to the new town of Lewiston. Others stayed on the boat and fought the rapids of the Snake, arriving perhaps a little later but in decidedly better shape than those who had sojourned in Walla Walla and experienced the decidedly bibulous and libidinous diversions that this frontier town provided so liberally.

Till 1859 steamboating had generally been a small business with individual captains owning their own boats and even doing a good share of the crew work. But in December 1860 a corporation was born that would have a distinct effect on the transportation picture on the River and with its corporate descendants dominate it for a greater length of the time than steamboats operated on the Lower and Upper Columbia. The Oregon Steam Navigation Company (ONC) was formed from the union of the Columbia River Navigation Company with the Oregon Transportation Company, and in a short time— some say because of the piratical business tactics common to the time and which the Company elevated to fine art—had a virtual monopoly on steamboat traffic on the Lower and Middle Columbia.

The new company couldn't have come on the scene at a better time. The interior, as the result of the Orofino and Cariboo gold strikes, was booming. New towns sprang up overnight as some of the miners who had gone to the gold fields discovered gold in another form: wheat. The bunchgrass land of Eastern Washington and Western Idaho, it was soon discovered, was some of the world's best dry-land wheat farming country; and in a decade, fields of rippling wheat were pouring a flood of gold into the new land and, via the River, to the world.

That wheat, to be effectively utilized, had to go to urban centers, first to the burgeoning new cities of the West Coast, and in time to the more heavily populated East. The key was transportation and the Oregon Steam Navigation Com-

pany was ready, willing, and able to furnish it . . . for a price. It was also at first the only organization able to haul a volume cargo in the territory, and in those days before monopolies were outlawed, that meant squeezing every last possible cent out of every ton-mile. The howls of anguished protest went unanswered if not unheard, and the ONC became undoubtedly one of the most profitable businesses in the United States.

To its credit, it must be admitted that the ONC provided good service and kept its fleet of handsome new white steamers in excellent repair. Some of the captains attained the status of genuine folk heroes and had their own devoted following who would never think of braving the

Until the backwaters of The Dalles Dam drowned it out, this canal provided riverboat traffic a safe passage around Celilo Falls.

Columbia with anyone else. Stacks of cordwood, at fifty cents a cord, dotted the landings and furnished an income for many a young man otherwise unemployed. Those stacks were often kept under armed guard, for the ONC's dominance of the river traffic did not go unchallenged. Every so often, a new company, tempted by the bonanza of swelling river trade, would take on the entrenched company, to be met by cut-rate fares and cut-throat tactics that would in a short time drive the newcomer into bankruptcy. The ONC would then magnanimously buy the challenger's steamers—at ten cents on the dollar—and promptly hike its rates to make up for the money it had lost in driving its competitor to the wall. Since capturing a competitor's fuel pile was the easiest way to put him out of business, it is easy to see why armed guards near woodpiles were more than an affectation.

In spite of the dangers inherent in the trade, becoming a riverman was the favorite dream of boys who grew up along the Columbia. Between 1860 and 1909, many of them realized that dream, for the Columbia was a busy commercial highway and carried most of the produce of the interior to the coastal seaports and the markets of the world.

The frantic trade of the gold rush days gradually died down and was replaced by the more mundane demands of the growing Inland Empire (the section of eastern Washington dominated by Spokane). While the Columbia River steamers never quite achieved the status of the plush floating bordellos of the Mississippi, there were nevertheless some very handsome excursion steamers plying the lower stretches of the River, especially from Portland to the Cascades through the splendors of the Columbia River Gorge. The Middle River stretches were devoted more to trade, although regular passenger service was maintained from Astoria to Kettle Falls. Above that, in Canadian waters, traffic was largely confined to commercial cargo, especially in refined ores traveling from the mines of Rossland to the smelter at Northport. That traffic died down somewhat after the establishment of the smelter at Trail, but it was soon replaced by increased traffic on the Arrow Lakes as that area began to develop. As late as 1953, a paddlewheel steamer ran a regular passenger service between Robson and Revelstoke; it has since been retired as a waterfront attraction on the beach at Nakusp.

The typical Columbia River steamer was of shallow draft, up to 220 feet long and, with few exceptions, a sternwheeler. Exceptionally maneuverable and of very tough construction, it was superbly adapted to the needs of its time and furnished one of the most colorful and romantic chapters in the history of the River. Toward the end of the steamboat era, the River saw some very well appointed craft, with comfortable accommodations and excellent meals. All in all, it was a very civilized method of transportation and one that is remembered with much nostalgia by those people who were fortunate enough to have experienced it.

The heyday of the steamer on the Columbia is usually reckoned from 1860 to 1909, when the railroads took over. Transferring freight at the Cascades, Celilo, and Kettle Falls was too expensive to make competition feasible, and so the colorful steamboat era ended, to be replaced some thirty years later by the more plebeian but efficient diesel-driven towboat and barge system. The Oregon Steam Navigation Company was sold in 1879 to the company controlled by Henry Villard, a German-born entrepreneur and while it continued in business as the Ore-

gon Railroad and Navigation Company, it was thereafter inextricably tied into and gradually absorbed by the system of railroads developing along the Columbia.

As early as 1850, there had been railroads of sorts around the falls at Cascade and between The Dalles and Celilo. These consisted of a rail system using mules as motive power, although a steam locomotive later did the pulling. The first real railroad in the Northwest operating between set points and on a regular schedule was the brainchild of that remarkable financier, promoter, and all-around entrepreneur, Dr. Dorsey S. Baker of Walla Walla.

First begun in 1869, this thirty-mile run from Wallula to Walla Walla was one of the most profitable enterprises in the Northwest, returning in one year almost as much as the entire road cost. It was also the source of many stories, some of them apocryphal, others all the more strange because they were absolutely true. The story that the early rails consisted of wooden stringers surfaced with rawhide, making traction on a wet day somewhat inefficient, and that in a hard winter the wolves would come down from the hills to feast on the right of way is simply not true, although after such a story was published in 1880 the railroad became known as "The Rawhide Railroad." What is true is that in 1872, before the road was completed all the way to Walla Walla and when capital was running short, the rails consisted of six-by-six-inch wooden stringers topped with a strip of strap iron two inches wide and three-eighths of an inch thick. These strips were securely fastened at the joints to keep them in place, but occasionally one of them would work loose and snap through the floor of the passing cars, much to the discomfiture of the passengers. These "snakeheads" were eliminated in 1875 when the road had generated enough income to replace the strap iron with narrow-gauge, wrought iron rails imported around the Horn from England. These diminutive rails carried an ever-increasing volume of freight till 1879, when the road was absorbed by the Villard interests and broadened to standard gauge.

The railroad-building fever of the 1860s spread to the Northwest as well as to all other parts of the country. Since the Columbia provided the only natural water-grade opening in the mountainous backbone of the West Coast, it was a foregone conclusion that the rails would follow the River, and so a lively contest developed for the right of way along the riverbanks. The Oregon Railway and Navigation Company was organized by Henry Villard, a shrewd and energetic railroad pioneer with a genius for high finance. He quickly realized that a line through the mountains along the Columbia would be a wedge between the Union Pacific in the south and the Northern Pacific to the north and so could largely influence both lines by interconnection. His railroad from Portland to Wallula was built at a furious pace and with such dangerous curves and tunnels that much of it had to be later rebuilt. The reason for the undue haste was that Villard hoped to divert the Northern Pacific System to the Columbia River and so make Portland rather than Puget Sound the western terminus of the northern transcontinental railway. In October 1883 the line was completed, and a tremendous party celebrated the seeming success of the venture.

The party turned out to be a bit premature. Northern Pacific interests, which had lost control of the road to Villard, cleverly jobbed the market, regained control, completed their line to Puget Sound, and made Tacoma the western terminus of the transcontinental road. It was a blow to Portland, and especially to Kalama, which had envisioned fantastic growth for itself as the tidewater terminus of the road. Nevertheless, a rail line along the Columbia existed and soon began carrying an impressive volume of freight, mostly at the expense of the steamboats.

The new railroad was soon connected to the Union Pacific system via the Oregon Short Line, and to the Southern Pacific via the Oregon and California Railroad. By 1910 the Columbia River was firmly integrated into the network of railways connecting the whole contiguous United States.

The Pacific Northwest has produced many flamboyant characters in its day but probably none more notable than Samuel Hill and his father-in-law, the empire-building James J. Hill. It is ironic that Sam Hill, himself a giant in his day, is usually referred to, but erroneously, as the son of Jim Hill, the Minnesotan whose epic battles with E. H. Harriman for control of the railroad empires of the Pacific Northwest provide the stuff from which many a regional legend is spun. Jim Hill planned to compete with his archrival, whose Union Pacific lines already reached to Portland along the south bank of the Columbia, by building a line along the north bank from Pasco to Vancouver. Harriman, act-

ing with characteristic speed and ruthlessness, chartered a couple of paper companies, bought rights of way, and laid tracks at every place where Hill's rails would have to go. Sometimes he succeeded and thus created legal roadblocks that slowed down the energetic Hill on his inexorable march to Vancouver. But he could not completely stop the Empire Builder. In time Hill triumphed and in 1908 his line, the Spokane, Portland and Seattle Railroad, was completed. It was said at the time that Hill utilized the time lost to Harriman's courtroom tactics to build the best constructed railroad in the United States; it kept his crews busy and eliminated the costly rebuilding that had been necessary on the south bank of the Columbia. But when Hill, flushed with his victory, announced that he was also planning to build a line along the Deschutes River to Bend, Harriman was neither amused nor deceived. Bend, at the time, consisted of a general store, a few saloons, and some scattered buildings—hardly a likely terminus for a line costing millions. It was, however, on a direct line to San Francisco, and Harriman instinctively knew that his hyperactive rival would never stop until the whistles of his locomotives echoed across the Golden Gate.

The fight for the Deschutes was probably the last of the great railroad wars, fought not only in the courtroom but more directly by gangs of tracklayers using fists, pick handles, rocks, and an occasional strategically placed charge of dynamite. Before it was over, all the expertise developed in forty years of railroad warfare had been brought to bear, and a few new twists peculiarly suited to this particular region had been introduced. Long-emplaced rocks mysteriously moved and crashed down onto the right of way. Wagonloads of supplies were routinely hijacked, and sharp-eyed sharpshooters using long-range buffalo guns with telescopic sights practiced on human targets on the far side of the canyon. The central plain of Oregon—a largely lawless land of stark, sun-baked basalt buttes, deep canyons, and rushing, rapid-filled rivers—echoed to gunfire and dynamite explosions as the representatives of the two most powerful railroad barons of the era used every means available to lay their own tracks and destroy those of their rivals.

The Harriman forces, by cleverly securing a vital right of way, finally forced the Hill interests to agree that they would not build past Bend but would be free to use the Union Pacific

This blunt-nosed towboat packs 3,000 horse-power in its compact frame and can push five loaded barges upstream.

A barge approaches the Columbia Gorge, which
often makes its own weather: in this case,
stormy.

trackage beyond that point. The warring gangs regretfully ended their feud, which had probably provided them with more diversion in their arduous march across the Central Oregon desert than anything else, and either drifted away or settled down on the land they had helped to open up. Jim Hill never lived to see the completion of his line to Bend: that distinction was reserved for Sam Hill, who inherited his father-in-law's dominant position in the railroad system the Empire Builder left behind as his legacy.

With such a father-in-law, Sam Hill must have been a frustrated man when he contemplated carving his own niche in the railroad empire to which he had entrée through his marriage to Mary, Jim Hill's eldest daughter. Jim Hill was definitely a tough act to follow. Sam, however, was cut from the same cloth as his father-in-law. Handsome, dynamic, accomplished, an indefatigable worker and consummate charmer, his job was more one of consolidation and development than pioneering. Through his efforts, the lines established by his father-in-law were developed and enlarged, and the full potential of the regions the elder Hill had tapped was realized. But brilliant as Sam Hill's accomplishments were in the field of railroading, they were eclipsed by two other marks he left on his beloved Pacific Northwest. One is the Museum of Fine Arts he endowed at Maryhill, the other is the legacy of good roads he left through his efforts for the Washington Good Roads Association.

SAM HILL WAS A complex, highly artistic person with an ingrained love of beauty . . . in any form. Of the thousands of acres he controlled, his favorite tract was the seven thousand acres in Skamania County opposite Biggs, and there he formalized in stone and concrete a dream he had long cherished. He built a castle in the wilderness, and in it he housed the souvenirs of a lifetime of acquisition. Whether he built Maryhill as a home, a museum, or simply as an expression of some innate urge has never been completely established—that is one secret that Sam took with him to his grave—but there it stands today, incongruously perched on a ledge above a five-hundred-foot cliff, towering over as wildly beautiful a stretch of desert river as anyone could ever wish to see. Comparisons to the castles on the Rhine are inevitable, and indeed Maryhill may well have been inspired by the castles Sam Hill saw in his many forays through Europe. It was a place fit for a queen, and indeed a queen dedicated it. In 1926 Queen Marie of Rumania, one of Sam's many titled friends, formally opened it to the public.

Sam's wife, after whom the castle was presumably named, never saw the place and would have absolutely nothing to do with it.

Besides running a railroad, building castles, collecting foreign decorations, and chasing around the world, Sam had other diversions. One of the more productive ones was his help in founding and promoting the Washington Good Roads Association, to which he lent his not inconsiderable political clout and financial support. Although he was in the railroad business, Sam Hill was a farseeing individual who realized that the automobile and internal combustion engine would revolutionize travel patterns in the United States and the world. He saw them supplanting steamboats and even railroads as the prime mode of travel and knew that soundly conceived roads were an integral part of the transportation revolution that would transform the Northwest and the whole country. Nothing could better epitomize this than the famous Columbia River Highway.

Pioneers over the Old Oregon Trail had usually crossed the river below The Dalles and proceeded along the north bank, since the south bank, through the precipitous Columbia River Gorge, was beyond the road-building ability of the period. It was to be some two decades into the twentieth century before Sam Hill's dreams of a road through the Columbia River Gorge along the south side was realized.

I first saw the Columbia River Highway on January 5, 1946, sheathed in the shimmer and glow of a silver thaw. At that time it was a narrow, serpentine, two-lane road etched into the surface of the towering cliffs of the Columbia River Gorge, skirting deep canyons and alive to the thunder and crash of a dozen waterfalls which sheeted the road in treacherous black ice. It was undoubtedly one of the most beautiful and, under the circumstances, terrifying highways I have ever seen—and I have seen quite a few of the world's most spectacular highways. As a memorial plaque at a rest stop near Hood River testifies, the highway was built at least in part by "honor camp inmates"—in other words, convict labor. And, aided by skilled Italian stonemasons, they built beautifully. Graceful stone arches bridge hundreds of creeks, fragile-looking but sturdy stone balustrades fringe the cliffs, and the vistas of the Gorge are incomparable. For fifty miles through the splendors of the Columbia River Gorge, parts of which are still preserved today as a scenic highway, this road was the main road between Portland and the interior.

Today, Interstate 84, a water-level, four-lane superhighway, shares the south bank with the railroad lines that border the River from Portland to Pasco. On the Washington side, a more meandering but excellent highway extends from Vancouver to the Interstate Bridge at Umatilla, and travelers breeze along somewhat in excess of the fifty-five-miles-per-hour speed limit over the same terrain painfully traversed by their great-grandfathers on the Old Oregon Trail. A stream of heavy trucks moves the commerce of the Inland Empire, effortlessly bridging in a few hours the miles it took the pioneers weeks to travel. And on the River itself, a towboat with a string of barges may be moving eight thousand tons of wheat or petroleum on a slack-water lake, where a hundred and fifty years ago the buckskinned fur brigades shot the rapids in their high prowed, fur laden bateaux.

The rapids are no more. Gone is the white water, the romance, the peril. In their place is a steady, mundane, but reliable commerce, for from Lewiston to the sea the Columbia and its chief tributary, the Snake, are a series of slack-water pools over which diesel-powered towboats move ponderous barges laden with wheat, fertilizer, lumber, petroleum, and all the diverse needs of a growing and dynamic region.

With the coming of the dams, water traffic, once relegated to obscurity by the railroads and the internal combustion engine, took out a new lease on life. A diesel-powered towboat and a string of flat-bottomed barges may not be as romantic as a snow-white paddle wheeler with her tall stacks shooting sparks and her resonant whistle waking the echoes of Wallula Gap, but they are highly efficient and can move bulk cargo at a lower cost per ton-mile than any other form of transportation except a pipeline.

I got a first-hand look at how a towboat and barge operate on a memorable trip from Burbank to Portland and back as a guest on the *Captain Bob,* a handsome new towboat owned by the Tidewater Barge Lines. I saw how empty barges are deployed at an island staging ground and how full barges are winched together into one solid unit by hard-working deck hands who decidely have a way with heavy hawsers. The captain, high on his bridge, knows the river like the back of his hand and maneuvers his ungainly looking flotilla of barges along a sometimes narrow channel or neatly inserts the whole thing into a lock with only inches to spare.

Through the locks of McNary, along the desolate river to John Day, at The Dalles where there is a magnificent view of Mount Hood towering above the River, or at Bonneville where the scenery is so breathtaking that one is hard pressed to watch the passage through the locks, the whole trip is memorable, especially when one realizes that one is passing over drowned rapids, Celilo Falls, and islands where for uncounted centuries the Indians had buried their dead.

The life of a riverman is still exciting, though hardly as perilous as it once was. Accommodations on a large towboat are first rate: an excellent bed, hot showers, all the food you can comfortably eat, and good, entertaining company—for one art that has not perished since the days of the steamboats is that of storytelling. The work is hard but well paid and engenders a pride that is the lineal descendant of the pride endemic to those intrepid men who first braved the Columbia and made it their servant.

Now, as then, the Columbia is the highway to the sea.

The Columbia Gorge

WHILE THE SIGHT OF THE Columbia River Gorge evokes a different emotion in the mind of each person first seeing it, there is a common denominator threading through all the various reactions. The geologist is thrilled by this unique cross section through the backbone of a major mountain range, the botanist is amazed by the complexity of plant life nourished by the moist atmosphere, and the hiker finds himself in paradise surveying a maze of trails climbing the precipitous slopes. The common denominator is a feeling of awe that has overwhelmed even the most blasé viewer, from the early Oregon Trail pioneer to today's traveler on Interstate 84, for this spectacular slash through the heart of the Cascades is one the most awesomely beautiful sights on the face of this planet.

Millions of years ago, geologists tell us, the area that today comprises the main drainage of the Snake and Columbia rivers was an inland sea, separated from the Pacific by an unbroken range of low-lying hills. The waters reached the ocean by way of the Colorado River and the Gulf of California. Then tremendous upheavals

The Columbia Gorge, looking upriver from Cape Horn on the Washington side, is an enchanting vista even in the rain.

pushed up that range of hills into the Rockies, built the Cascades, and tilted and folded the bottom of this prehistoric sea; and the River had to find a new outlet to the sea.

It found it across the newly formed Horse Heaven Hills which were slowly rising from layers of still plastic basalt, through an opening now known as Wallula Gap. The new, young river had sufficient erosive power to keep ahead of the slowly rising barrier and eventually slam headlong into the Cascade Range. No one knows for certain how long it took the River to find the low spot in the mountain wall, but eventually it did, and the fast flowing waters, probably moving along a fissure opened by earthquakes, began forming their present channel.

The Cascades were also building at this time, but the erosive power of the river was able to keep up with them. In time cliffs arose along the River as the banks, pushed by incredibly great forces within the earth, rose higher and higher while the rocks and sand carried by the swiftly flowing torrent constantly deepened the channel.

And so it went for millions of years. Then, beginning about one hundred thousand years ago and ending as little as twenty thousand years ago, a different force began to shape the Columbia Gorge—ice.

Moving down from the Arctic as a ponderously slow but irresistible force, at least five advancing and receding ice sheets covered the northern part of Washington, Idaho, and Montana. Glaciers moved down the valleys, gouging them even deeper, covered all but the highest mountains, and dammed the flow of the Columbia and one of its main tributaries, the Clark Fork. A huge and very deep lake began to form behind this ice barrier, covering most of Northern Idaho and extending well into Montana. When the dam finally broke, it produced the greatest flood of which we have scientific proof.

Coursing across central Washington with a volume of nine cubic miles per hour, this deluge gouged out the Grand Coulee and laid bare the basaltic backbone of the central plateau. It also poured through the established opening in the Cascade mountains and, due to the peculiar segmented nature of basalt, tore out millions of tons of solid rock on its mad dash to the sea. Much of the topography of the Columbia Gorge as we know it today can be traced to that Great Spokane Flood.

The littoral of the River was changed several times by landslides, some of gigantic proportions. One of them, about seven hundred and fifty years ago, dammed the Columbia at Cascade Locks for several weeks, and when the river finally breached the barrier, it produced the Cascade Rapids, a major impediment to early navigation on the Columbia.

The Gorge is approximately fifty miles long, stretching roughly from Hood River to the Sandy River. Some say the beginning of the Gorge is nearer Mosier; indeed, at this point the cliffs are studded with oaks, and scenery begins to take on the spectacular qualities that are the hallmark of the Gorge. Multishaded rock strata on either side of the River show the folding and banding action that raised the Cascades, and they afford geologists an exciting look into the very heart of the mountains. But at Hood River the cliffs are suddenly clad in conifers, the walls of the Gorge become precipitous, and the River is enclosed in a narrow, stony corridor through which it will flow for the next fifty miles.

The Indians regarded the Gorge with awe liberally laced with superstition, and many of the local legends are founded on geological features of the place. At the head of the Gorge sits Memaloose Island, the Island of the Dead, the most prominent of the many island burial grounds, where for centuries the Indians had deposited their dead, surrounded by the things they would need in the afterlife. Memaloose Island is largely buried in the impounded waters of Lake Bonneville now, but when the early pioneers first came to this country it was a sacred and eerie place, with every nook and cranny of its craggy surface occupied by swathed, often seated cadavers brooding in eternal silence over the rapids that had provided their sustenance during life.

Travelers on Interstate 84 and Washington 14 who use the elaborate camping and resting areas that overlook this site are often puzzled by the sight of a stone obelisk at the west end of the island. This definitely non-Indian burial marker marks the final resting place of Vic Trevitt, an early Oregon pioneer and admirer of the Indians who, after many years of association with them, declared them to be the most honest people along the Columbia. On Judgment Day, he often said, he'd take his stand with the Indians; and so, when he passed away, and according to his wishes, his remains were interred on Memaloose Island. An old postcard shows his monument surrounded with the skulls, femurs, and tibia of his deceased friends, among whom he presumably found his final peace. When the waters impounded behind Bonneville Dam buried a great part of Memaloose Island, the Indian remains were reburied elsewhere, but Vic Trevitt's obelisk still remains, a mute yet eloquent reminder that not all pioneers of the Old Oregon Trail saw in the original inhabitants of this beautiful region an implacable foe.

One of the most persistent legends of the region is that of the Bridge of the Gods. This legend may well have sprung from the bridging of the Columbia by a huge landslide near Cascade Locks for which there is irrefutable scientific proof. The other more romantic but equally plausible source of the legend is that held by every regional Indian tribe: that the Columbia was once bridged by a natural stone arch and that over this convenient highway the tribes passed back and forth across the River.

Modern geologists seem to be divided as to whether this arch actually existed. Those who think it did point out that a heavy flow of dense basalt resting on a pocket of volcanic ash and scoria deposited by a previous eruption could have been undermined by the pressure of the raging river, and so form an arch under which the swiftly flowing torrent would have quickly dug a deep channel. They believe this could have happened in the immediate vicinity of the present Bridge of the Gods; and indeed, fathometer readings in the river indicate the presence of large masses of rock at right angles to the current. Opponents of this theory counter with "Show me the abutments," which to date have not been positively identified.

Still, anyone familiar with the way legends are handed down from father to son among Indian tribes has much respect for their authenticity. And the legend is a charming one. Thousands of years ago, it recalls, two strong chiefs lived on opposite sides of the Columbia. Their tribes freely passed back and forth over the Columbia over a great natural stone bridge, and the chiefs became great friends, hunting and fishing together. They even vowed eternal friendship between themselves and their people. As long as that friendship endured, the legend said, the bridge would stand, remaining strong and solid. But both chiefs became enamored of the same lovely maiden and their friendship became rivalry, finally erupting into warfare. The great god Coyote, hating to see such a bitter ending to what had been a beautiful friendship, changed one chief into craggy Mount Hood, the other into massive Mount Adams, and the Indian maid into beautiful Mount St. Helens, where each could see the other but be forever apart. And true to the prophecy, the bridge crashed into the Columbia.

Modern scientists who believe in the arch legend have a more prosaic explanation. They believe the arch fell about five thousand years ago, during the violent earthquakes that were prevalent when Hood, Adams, and St. Helens were active or semiactive volcanoes.

LEWIS AND CLARK, on their epic journey to the sea, wax lyrical in their descriptions of the Gorge. A deep castellated slash through the heart of the Cascade Mountains, it still evokes the same emotions today, for this is one portion of the River that is relatively unchanged. The sheer cliffs, their tops crowned with giant firs and hemlocks, the crashing waterfalls tumbling hundreds of feet from the ice fields of Mount Hood, the soft moist climate that nurtures a veritable jungle of plant life, all these are practically the same as they were two centuries ago. What is different are the roads bordering each side of the river, and the busy stream of railroad and river traffic using the River night and day, for the Gorge is not only a scenic wonderland, but also an integral part of the busy highway to the sea that is the Columbia River.

Because of the precipitous nature of the Gorge, it has largely escaped the urbanization which has blighted so many other scenic areas. At its head, the town of Hood River spreads up a narrow valley, while on the Washington side the town of Bingen clings to the river bank very much like its namesake on the Rhine. A mile above Bingen, the pretty town of White Salmon perches on a high bench, affording a spectacular view of Mount Hood and the River flowing through its surrounding phalanx of cliffs. In the Gorge itself, Cascade Locks on the south side and Stevenson on the north are the only town of any size, although the newly relocated towns of North Bonneville, next to the second powerhouse at Bonneville Dam, may someday grow into its projected platting and become a fairly

Many of the most beautiful vistas of the Columbia River Gorge are best viewed from the less travelled Washington side of the River.

The Columbia Gorge is a wonderland of waterfalls and shady glens, one of the most beautiful spots on this planet.

From Vista Point, the viewer is treated to a magnificent view of the entrance to the scenic Columbia River Gorge.

large town. Certainly no place is more scenically located or lavishly laid out.

The towering cliffs along the south side of the Gorge made a road along that side not only very difficult to build but, once achieved, also tremendously scenic. Part of the Old Columbia Highway is still preserved as a scenic route, and on a summer day it carries almost as much traffic as the freeway, even though its effective speed is about twenty-five miles an hour. This is hardly a road for anyone in a hurry, but then anyone electing to take this route does so because of the beauty around every bend and curve of the serpentine road, and not to get from the Sandy River to Cascade Locks in a hurry. It is a road through a tunnel of overhanging trees, under towering, often dripping cliffs, and alive with the sound of falling water. It is a journey through which the sunlight filters in an ever-changing mosaical pattern of green and gold, broken occasionally by a breathtaking vista of river, sky, and mountains as the road snakes from one spectacular view to another, each one seemingly the ultimate in beauty until it is eclipsed by the next. It is no wonder that people who have traveled the whole world rate the Columbia Gorge as one of the greatest sights this planet affords.

Probably one of the greatest attractions of the Gorge is that it is never twice the same. Changes of seasons, light, or weather give each day a difference, so that no one ever has a chance to become bored with it. It presents one face in spring, when it comes to life in a burst of verdant green, and it reaches a seeming climax of beauty in summer, when it is clothed in a full set of luxuriant foliage, only to be eclipsed in autumn, when the vine maple and poplar interspersed through the more somber conifers put on a veritable riot of color. But for sheer awesome beauty, one should see the Gorge sheeted in a silver thaw, with the sun glinting on a billion diamonds, creating a kaleidoscope of color, or clothed in the glistening ermine of sunlight on newly fallen snow. Even in the rain and mist, when the trees become an array of shaggy ghosts that are downright unreal, the Gorge is a paradox of beauty, for this beauty can also be deadly.

People familiar with the Gorge will tell you that it makes its own weather, and this is largely true. The funneling effect of a break in the mountain chain forces wind through the gorge at a greater than average velocity. Ice can form here when it forms nowhere else, and snow is a natural occurrence in the Gorge when the area around it is largely snow free. Prevailing upriver winds have beaten the trees in that direction and regularly drive the rain into the terrain with such force that slides are common in the gorge. It is a region of awesome beauty but also a region where all the forces of Nature are magnified, as if to exact some toll for the beauty so extravagantly manifested here.

For many years the only method of travel through the Gorge was a perilous journey by boat: the banks were much too precipitous for a conventional road. With the coming of the railroads, the impossible became the imperative, and so a roadbed was painstakingly constructed along the south bank, often clinging by the barest margin of safety to a rock bench blasted into the face of a vertiginous cliff or boring through headlands in a series of tunnels. It was perilous work on a roadbed ballasted with gold, but if the price was high, so was the reward of success, and in time the road was completed. For many years it was the only practical method of moving a volume of goods overland through the Columbia Gorge.

The challenge of building a highway through the Gorge could not long be ignored by the likes of railroad king Sam Hill, lumber baron Simon Benson, or businessman John Yeon—men to whom overwhelming odds were the very spice of life. It was only natural that they would implement the plans to build an all-weather highway along the Oregon side of the Gorge. First begun in 1912, the road was built in bits and pieces, and partly by "honor men" detailed by the governor. Some say these were convicts allowed to work out their sentences by doing useful work, others say "honor men" were highly placed citizens who donated their time and energy to the project. One old man who worked on the project recalls that the stone work was entrusted to Italian stonemasons who may not have been too fluent in English but certainly communicated their artistic talents well with basalt. Separate camps were set up for each ethnic group, for at this time the "melting pot" was still bubbling and each group felt more at ease with people who spoke their own particular language. Still, all these diverse elements somehow coordinated their efforts so that by 1924 all the pieces had been connected and an all-weather road ran along the south side of the Columbia from Portland to The Dalles.

People traveling this road often think that it was intentionally laid out as a scenic highway, so perfectly does it exploit every vista, every wooded dell, every waterfall. Actually, it simply follows the most logical line of least resistance, although one could easily believe that the engineer who designed it secretly had the soul of a poet.

The high spot of the road is Crown Point, built in 1917 and first reviled by its detractors as "The Million Dollar Outhouse." Built on a high cliff overlooking the whole gorge, it commands unquestionably one of the finest scenic views in the United States . . . or the world. In a series of sweeping curves, the road descends closer to river level past a series of lacy waterfalls draining from the ice fields of Mount Hood. This area was logged off long ago, but vestiges of the original old growth forests still lend an air of majesty to an already superlatively beautiful scene. The new growth, now quite respectable in size, is mostly deciduous maple and alder that make a leafy tunnel of the curvy road. Although there are a few private homes along the way, the route is largely clothed in forest and the abundant flora that makes the Gorge a botanist's paradise.

A surprising variety of plant growth flourishes in the Gorge. Because of the turbulence of the streams, evaporation is high, but the waters reach the Columbia still in their pristine purity and frigidity. Plants are often found next to the cold streams that would normally be more at home in the Arctic tundra. The explanation is quite simple. A thermometer held six inches from a mountain stream on a warm summer day will register a temperature more appropriate to winter, and for that reason the Gorge is a cool haven from the sultry days that sometimes occur even in normally air-conditioned Oregon and Washington. Wahkeena Falls, for example, always has a current of cool air flowing along its tumultuous water course and even on the hottest day is a delightful refuge that refreshes the body with its cold water, the ear with its bubbling chatter, the eye with its shimmering play of light and shadow, and the soul with its overall beauty.

A series of strategically placed parks helps exploit the full beauty of the Gorge by making it accessible to many people. Some of them, such as Ainsworth, have full camping and picnicking facilities, while water-level parks such as Rooster Rock cater more to a water-sports-oriented crowd. This park, incidentally, is named euphemistically from a saltier and much more descriptive name bestowed by the early river men on a large upright rock that dominates the west end of the preserve. The island adjacent to the park, Sand Island, is a favorite retreat of overnight campers and nudists, a mix which can and often does lead to comic overtones, for each group, in its own way, is enjoying the beauties of the Gorge.

Nowhere in its full course is the diversity of the Columbia more evident than in the Columbia Gorge. On its entrance it is a desert river. It soon reenters the wooded realm it last saw in Canada and in fifty miles is transformed into a tidal river. At its upper end, a semi-arid vegetation prevails. In the depths of the Gorge, it is rainfall forest vegetation that predominates; and at its end, the flora that the river will wear clear to the ocean first manifests itself. It is almost as though the River, having overcome its last major barrier to the sea, were triumphantly showing off its versatility in a last burst of scenic splendor and bestowing its bounty of beauty as a gracious gesture before it becomes a sedate stream flowing peacefully to its mating with the sea.

The Columbia is everywhere beautiful, but here in the Gorge it rises to heights of sublimity. No one can ever view it without remembering it as one of the great experiences of a lifetime.

It is a fit tribute to the Great River of the West.

Salmon Forever?

WHEN LEWIS AND CLARK made their epochal journey of discovery, they were under orders from President Thomas Jefferson to make note not only of geographical features of the country they were exploring, but also of the fauna and flora. This they faithfully did: their journals bulge with descriptions of new plants and exotic life species, many of them hitherto unknown to the inhabitants of the East Coast. All were described in great detail and with occasional footnotes of how the new species could be put to some useful purpose in the settlement of the new regions which, they foresaw, would inevitably occur.

Nothing impressed them more, took up a greater part of their journals, or was described in greater detail than the life cycle, harvest, and economic potential of the Pacific salmon. And justly so, for just as the American bison, the buffalo, was the staff of life to the Plains Indians, so the Pacific salmon was the mainstay of the tribes adjacent to the Great River of the West. Theirs was a salmon economy. The

Sports fishermen are taking an ever increasing toll of a rapidly diminishing species. These boats are part of the flotilla working out of Westport, Washington.

migrations of these anadromous fish governed the life of the tribes, most of their customs and religious customs were built around them, and their everyday activities centered around the harvest and preparation of the fish that would sustain them for yet another year.

When John Cabot came to Newfoundland in 1497, he found the streams teeming with the Atlantic salmon, with which he was familiar since it also inhabited the streams of Scandinavia and the British Isles. This fish spawns in fresh water and then returns, exhausted but still alive, to the ocean to return again for another round of breeding. Not so the Pacific salmon.

There are four kinds of salmon of economic importance inhabiting the rivers of the Pacific Northwest, Canada, and Alaska. Of these, unquestionably the chinook or king salmon, by reason of its great size, is most important. Specimens five feet long and a weight of sixty pounds or more are not unusual. The smaller silver salmon, usually weighing about a tasty twelve pounds, is much sought after not only as a commercial but also as a game fish, while the sockeye is of great importance in British Columbia and Alaska, where it often constitutes the greater part of the annual run. The humpback is the least desirable of the four species and, as its common nickname (dog salmon) would indicate, was formerly considered as food fit only for dogs. All are anadromous fish, born in fresh water, growing to maturity in the sea, and returning to their parent stream for spawning. The one big difference between the Atlantic and the Pacific salmon is that the Pacific salmon almost invariably dies after spawning, unless it can reach salt water, in which case it survives as a biological curiosity. But as a general rule, spawning is the last convulsive, magnificent climax to a life cycle of about four years, three of which are spent in the ocean.

The salmon begins life as a larva wriggling tail first out of its sand- and gravel-covered nest with a yolk sac still attached. This happens in January, but by March the larvae have grown to free-swimming fry and by fall are fingerlings five or six inches long. Drawn by some primordial instinct, they begin the long journey to the Pacific, a journey fraught with many perils not only from the natural predators to whom plump six-inch-long salmon are a choice delicacy, but also from technological perils built in their road to the sea by man.

To an engineer, water cascading unused over a dam spillway is energy gone to waste. The demand for hydrologically generated energy is such that every drop of water that can logically be used to generate electricity is run though a turbine, and this is usually the same route a fingerling takes to reach the sea . . . if he's lucky. The sudden pressure changes encountered when the small fish is sluiced through a turbine often ruptures its air bladder, making it easy prey for the ubiquitous scavenging sea gulls lurking below every dam.

If water is being spilled over the dam, the fingerling faces another, more subtle danger. Water plunging into the deep pool below the dam carries with it a large quantity of entrapped air. Nitrogen dissolves into the water, and the fish, breathing this saturated mixture, develops nitrogen narcosis ("the bends") which, if not fatal, is debilitating enough to make the young fingerling an easy meal for the many predators waiting for it on its way to the sea. Another danger is pollution pouring from industrial plants and towns along the river, although in the last few years this danger has been considerably alleviated due to the stringent ecological controls a newly aware society has imposed. Then, there are always other, bigger fish and land predators to whom young salmon are a tasty treat. It is a wonder any fingerlings ever reach the ocean to grow to maturity, but enough of them do to keep the salmon run, if not up to the prodigious numbers of the pioneer days, at least more or less intact.

In the ocean, the salmon grows rapidly, becoming in three years a sleek, silvery piscatorial torpedo nearly four feet long, vibrant with power and filled with the urge to reproduce its kind. Moved by some as yet unexplained instinct, it leaves the ocean and begins a journey that can exceed a thousand miles to its parent stream. Once there, it moves up to usually the very spot where it was born. The journey may take many months, and by the time the female salmon has reached the spot where she will lay her eggs, she is a pathetic shadow of the sleek fish that left salt water. Covered with fungus, her fins battered and torn, she still has energy enough to scoop out a nest in the gravel of a shallow, swift flowing stream with powerful strokes of her tail. There she deposits her hundreds or even thousands of pea-sized eggs. Swimming behind her, an equally battered male, his lower jaw grown into a grotesque hook, impregnates the newly laid eggs with a milky male sperm substance known as milt; and the fertilized eggs, if they escape the not-so-tender mercies of the voracious trout usually lurking nearby, will be buried by the sand washed down by the swift stream. Some three months later, the larvae will emerge, one more link in a cyclical chain reaching back eons.

The parent fish, exhausted and weak from the long struggle upstream and the protracted fast they have both endured since leaving the sea, usually die within the day. On the upper Salmon and Snake rivers, the stench of decaying carcasses pervades the air, and bears and eagles grow fat on the remains of what had been one of the most magnificent fishes ever created. It seems a cruel and unnecessary waste, but it is a system that has functioned in a beautifully balanced rhythm for millions of years. Now, that rhythm may have been artificially altered by man to the point that the Pacific salmon has already been greatly depleted. Its continued existence, if not endangered, has been at least seriously threatened.

When the white man first came to the Pacific Northwest, the quantities of salmon teeming in the streams tributary to the Columbia River could only be described in numbers usually associated with astronomy. Small streams were literally choked with the fish during the spring and fall runs, so that it would have been possible to walk across the stream on the backs of the salmon, if only they would stand still for it. Their sheer numbers made them easy prey, even to the comparatively crude fishing implements of the Indians living along the Great River, to whom they were a staple of life. Caught in great numbers at the height of their migrations, they were dried, often stacked like cordwood, and were a prime item of commerce. The arrival of the first salmon was a cause of much jubilation, and elaborate rites to placate the spirit of Salmon were performed. The Indians respected the salmon, rightfully according it a place of honor in their lives, for without the silvery horde, life along the Great River would not have been as pleasant or as easy as it was.

The earliest white explorers, who at once realized that the whole food economy of the region was built around the salmon, also realized that there was a tremendous economic potential in these swarming hordes of silvery fish. Nathaniel Wyett's first efforts to export Columbia River salmon to the world ended in disaster because of technological shortcomings, but later efforts, especially during the Civil War when vast quantities of nonperishable food were required, resulted in the founding of the canning industry on the Columbia River. Advanced canning methods, whereby sections of the fish were cooked and packed into a hermetically sealed metal can, made it possible to export salmon to the whole world. Almost overnight, canneries sprang up along the River and thousands of workers who had finished building the transcontinental railways went to work canning the seemingly limitless bounty of the Columbia.

News of the bonanza on the River soon reached Europe, and whole colonies of new immigrants with innate fishing instincts soon sprang up. Usually quite chauvinistic, they kept to themselves, keeping their own languages and customs and intermingling only when absolutely necessary. Astoria became a mostly Finnish stronghold, while Clifton had colonies of Greeks, Yugoslavs, and Italians, all staying pretty much to themselves and zealously guarding what they considered their own territories. The ubiquitous fish knife was certainly no affectation: it was an everyday tool that was also worn at the Saturday night dance, where it all too often was used to slice up something other than fish. Small villages, usually perched on the river bank and accessible only by boat, sprang up. Usually built around a cannery, they were self-contained units in which the life of every resident centered on salmon.

With fish spears and crude cedar bark nets, the Indians had harvested only the salmon they needed for personal sustenance or intertribal trade, and they made no discernible impact on the salmon run. The white man introduced new, more efficient methods of fishing, including the purse seine, huge horse-drawn nets, and the gill net. Probably the most brutal device of all was the fish wheel, a water-powered wheel with pocket-like nets, which was so efficient that it threatened to catch all the fish in the Columbia until it was outlawed by common consent in 1927. These methods of capture began to make inroads in the salmon run almost immediately, but such were the incredible numbers of fish in the Columbia that it was some years before the diminution of the salmon run became noticeable. The lower Columbia was fringed with picturesque fishing villages, the canneries worked around the clock during the fishing season, and Columbia River salmon became an economical and staple item on the pantry shelves of the American household.

For almost forty years, salmon was king on the lower Columbia. Then, the first of the large dams, Bonneville, was built, to be soon followed by Grand Coulee, which had no fish ladders and so cut off the whole Canadian sector of the River as breeding streams. In rapid succession other dams were built on the River: McNary, Chief Joseph, The Dallas, John Day, Rocky Reach, Wanapum, Priest Rapids and, finally, in 1967, Wells Dam, the last dam on the River to have fish ladders. Then, too, the rapid industrialization brought on by World War II began to pour pollutants into what had been a largely unpolluted stream, and urban development along the River contributed to an ever-increasing amount of largely untreated sewage. Faced with these new ecological hazards, the salmon run plunged sharply. It was the beginning of the end for a most colorful chapter in the Columbia's history, for little by little the riverside canneries became inoperative, their satellite villages became ghost towns, and what was left of the industry become centralized in Astoria. There were fewer fish every year and what was left was subjected not only to an intensified fishing program from commercial fishermen now concentrated near the River's mouth, but also by an ever-increasing army of sports fishermen whose previously negligible inroads now became a drain of serious proportions. And this brings us up to the present.

When the great hydrological projects on the Columbia were in the planning stage, much thought was given to the problem of perpetuating, as much as possible, the salmon run on the Columbia. The Lower and Middle River dams up to Chief Joseph were constructed with fish ladders, a series of comparatively small waterfalls which the powerful salmon could leap with ease. Much research on the life pattern of the salmon was done, and hatcheries that hopefully would offset the effects of the dams were planned as an integral part of the whole operation. Millions of fish were planted in salmon-bearing streams to offset the mortality that engineers knew would be inevitable when the young fingerlings migrated to the sea through the spinning turbines of the massive generators, or over the spillways into the nitrogen-saturated pools below the dams.

Has it worked? Well, there is still a salmon run on the Columbia, although it is sadly depleted from the days when a person could drive a wagon hub deep into a stream full of migrating salmon and, simply by passing his pitchfork haphazardly through the stream, fill that wagon with impaled fish in a very short time. The slack-water pools behind the impoundments have proved to be a larger obstacle than the rapids of the free-flowing river ever were. The slowly flowing water picks up heat more readily, forms algae more easily, and becomes a haven for hordes of voracious carp that decimate the fingerling run. Opponents to the dams refer to them as "biological deserts" as far as spawning beds are concerned, and this is largely true, since salmon need swiftly flowing water for proper breeding grounds. In the whole 1,264 miles of the River, only a sixty-mile stretch of water above the headwaters of McNary Dam now qualifies as breeding grounds, and even this will disappear if the proposed Ben Franklin Dam is ever constructed. Year by year, the run diminishes and what is left is subjected to ever-increasing pressure.

THE TREATY OF 1855 with the tribes living along the Columbia and its tributaries specifically guarantees the Indians the right to fish "at their usual and accustomed places." The tribes have jealously guarded this right and probably have gained almost as much in court as they lost at the treaty table. The famous Boldt decision, guaranteeing the Indians 50 percent of the available catch, was greeted with stunned astonishment by non-Indian commercial fishermen who claimed it would ruin them, and often it was openly defied by rifle-toting fishermen not accustomed to backing away from any fight. The decision has been appealed and upheld by the United States Supreme Court.

At present, fish canning activities center at Astoria. Individual fishermen sell their catch either directly to a cannery or to fish buyers who act as agents for the packers and the distributors of fresh fish. Prices for salmon have escalated to the point that what used to be a commonly used household staple is now a gourmet delicacy . . . and priced accordingly. Filling the void are varieties of fish scorned by the early packers but which now find a ready market. Not so long ago, ling cod, an ugly but delicious bottom fish, was considered a nuisance; today, it can mean the difference between a good run and one that barely pays expenses.

The second most important food fish of the Columbia is the white sturgeon, a fish that evolved forty million years ago and has survived practically unchanged simply because it is so well adapted to its environment that no change is necessary. A horny-plated, vacuum-mouthed bottom feeder that can grow to over ten feet in length and exceed one thousand pounds in weight, it is a delicacy more and more in demand by the American public. A cousin, the Caspian Sea sturgeon, is already famous as the producer of that gourmet delicacy, caviar. Shad, halibut, and assorted bottom fish round out the Columbia fisherman's yearly take, from which he can make, in a good year, a comfortable but hard-earned living.

The most commonly used method of fishing in the Columbia is gill netting. This consists of a 1,500-foot net anchored at one end and payed out from a boat at the other. Usually about forty feet in width, the net is made of tough nylon cord. Depending on the season and the fish for which it is intended, openings are either a six- or eight-inch rectangle, through which a salmon pokes its head, finds it cannot swim through, and tries to back out, only to be imprisoned by its gills catching in the net cords. It is a highly efficient method of fishing, because smaller fish swim unimpeded through the openings, and any fish that is caught usually is of legal size. Payed out across a suitable stretch of river up which fish are migrating, the net usually becomes heavy with entrapped salmon in a matter of a few hours or even minutes. When the fisherman feels he has a suitable catch, he hauls in his net, either over a hydraulically assisted roller at the bow of his boat (a *bowpicker*) or over the stern with a large

A gillnetter working from a small boat lands a salmon that has become entangled in his net. Both fisherman and salmon are somewhat endangered species.

drum that operates by hydraulics on power from his engine. As the fish come in, the net is cleared and stored either in the bottom of the boat or on the stern. After the full 1,500 feet of netting has been hauled in, the net is payed out again to await another catch. It used to be that gill netting was done only at night because by day the fish, seeing the net, would avoid it. With the advent of nylon, which is practically invisible in water, daylight fishing became practical and now accounts for most of the catch.

Through trial and error, a special craft suitable for this type of work has evolved. The usual Columbia River bowpicker is about twenty feet long, very high in the bow and stern to weather the waves of the Columbia Bar, and practically unsinkable. A small cabin sits well aft, usually with a chimney sticking out and emanating wood smoke and the smell of hot coffee. Accommodations are minimal although some of the older bowpickers have bunks where the two-person crew can catch a few winks if the fishing is slow. Most of the boats have a hydraulically assisted roller at the bow over which the net is hauled, but some of the real old timers do it the hard way: hard hands grasping the net and painfully hauling it in, hand over hand, until the whole net has been cleared. No wonder it took tough men to man the old bowpickers: it was tough work, and after twenty years of it, any man, no matter how strong, looked and felt old.

The modern sternpickers are quite a different matter. Sleek, efficient, redolent of power, they easily spool their 1,500-foot nets off large drums set on the afterdeck and have taken most of the back-breaking work out of fishing, although enough remains to still qualify it as very hard work. The enclosed cabin is snug, weatherproof, and houses a bewildering array of electronic gadgets: radar, radio compass, ship-to-shore radios, fathometers, all-electric galleys, refrigerator, comfortable beds, and even an occasional built-in bar. As can be imagined, this type of boat, with its powerful engines and sophisticated gear, represents a considerable investment, but a boat of this type having a good run can pay for itself in a season or two. Since their range is considerable and they are large enough to be very seaworthy, Columbia River sternpickers occasionally venture as far as Alaska, although they usually make the trip as some freighter's deck cargo. It is not unusual for a boat of this type to have a whole family aboard; and one boat that I know of, representing a better-than-half-million-dollar investment, even has a built-in mother-of-pearl shrine! The investment, however, is usually around fifty thousand dollars. An old bowpicker could be picked up for perhaps five thousand dollars, and this is the way the new fisherman gets started, gradually working his way up the equipment line as his credit rating escalates. It's tough, hard work, but to a dedicated fisherman with salt water in his veins, it is the most natural way on earth to earn a living.

Astoria is still largely a fishing town. It is evident in the appearance of the people: tanned, powerful men with work-hardened hands and eyes squinted from habit against the glare of the sun on the water. Finnish, Italian, Greek, and Yugoslavian sounding names are common, all owned by good Americans fiercely proud of their heritage and determined to preserve it.

This determination has crystallized in concerted efforts, ecological and political, to preserve the salmon run that is the mainstay of their way of life. These men are fishermen and don't want to be anything else. They view with alarm the steady depletion of the salmon run, but their sons and daughters still look to the River as their ultimate place of employment. Even while they decry the decline of the salmon population, they prepare themselves for lives as fishermen, for way back in their minds is the unshakable hope that the Columbia, the grandest salmon river on Earth, will always have a viable run of fish. A Columbia River without a salmon run would be unthinkable, and to most of these young people, fishing is the most natural job on Earth.

There is one large and growing group of people who fervently hope that this is true. There always have been people who have fished the Columbia not for profit, but for the sheer fun of it, and this group has grown over the years into a formidable bloc determined to preserve the fish run in the Columbia at any costs, even if it means severely limiting commercial fishing. Sports fishermen formerly took only a very small part of the total run, but their numbers have grown so large and their pursuit of salmon and steelhead so intense that today they account for a considerable portion of all the fish taken from the Columbia. Around the mouth of the Columbia where salmon are still avidly feeding before their long trek up the river, the sportsmen's quarry is mostly salmon. Farther up the river, they also seek the steelhead trout, an overgrown rainbow that went to sea and there grew to three feet or more of fighting fury. Like the salmon, it is an anadromous fish, born in fresh water, migrating to the sea, and returning to the fresh water in which it was born for spawning. Unlike the salmon, the steelhead does not necessarily die from this act and will take a lure while on its spawning trip – a factor which makes it an avidly sought quarry by legions of cold, runny-nosed steelhead addicts who are having the time of their lives. The tributaries of the Columbia – among them the Snake, Salmon, Clearwater, and Grande Ronde – are famous steelhead streams and even during the cold winter months are the targets of thousands of avid steelheaders to whom the pursuit of this fish is the finest sport on earth.

Steelhead thrive on clear, fast-running water, and so to them the slack-water pools behind the dams are simply long stretches of tedious traveling that must be passed if they are to reach the fast, clear streams they call home. Back in the days when the Columbia was one more or less continuous rapid, steelhead and salmon spawned all along the length of the stream. The dams changed all that, and now a fish may travel well over twelve hundred miles to satisfy its primordial reproductive urge.

When Dworshak Dam on the North Fork of the Clearwater was built, it cut off one of the finest steelhead spawning streams in the world. To compensate for this, the U.S. Army Corps of Engineers established a hatchery near Orofino. Here millions of steelhead fingerlings are raised to viable size, then released in the river just as though they had been born in the North Fork. Three or four years later, steelhead trout three feet long fight their way up the pipe through which they were originally released. It works, all right, but at a tremendous cost in attrition of fish, for of the millions released only a small percentage survive the turbines, the gulls, and the predator fish to return to their natal points. Still, it is a sign of what can be, and the fact that successful salmon and steelhead runs have been reestablished in streams previously cleared of these fish is an encouraging precedent that has not gone unnoticed. As more and more attention is given to ecology, it is safe to assume that this aspect of the Columbia's life will be safeguarded not only as a vitally needed industrial and food resource, but also as a recreational asset of tremendous value.

A grizzled old Finn at Astoria, his blunt fingers calloused from years of pulling gill nets, put it to me in his own inimitable way: "Fishin'," he said, in his strongly accented speech, "is mos' natural way for men to make a livin'. Dese fish be here long after we gone. Fish an' dis river, dey go togedder. Always be fish in Columbia and always be people like me to ketch dem."

Maybe he's right. Fish and the Columbia do go together. It is a natural part of the Columbia River's overall picture for it to have a strong and viable run of fish, and for man to tamper with this system to the point of extinction would be the rank folly. Much of the criticism by white men against the Boldt decision had centered around the Indian's alleged abuse of their fishing rights. After a big haul, they will tell you, an Indian is apt to go on a glorious spree and leave his nets untended for a couple of weeks, while thousands of entrapped salmon rot in them. I checked on this with an Indian fisherman, a leader of his tribe, who admitted that while the story may have occasionally been true, it would be highly unlikely nowadays, partly because of the high price of salmon, but mostly because the Indians, aware of the criticisms that would adversely affect their treaty rights in a court decision, are policing their own people, and most effectively. An Indian leaving his nets untended for more than twenty-four hours is liable to censure and very positive action from his own tribe, but also to a far more effective control measure: someone else will harvest his salmon, and he will have no redress.

No one, not even the most convinced optimist, will claim that the fishing problems of the Columbia are not manifold or that they will be solved overnight. The problems are many and complex, but the fact that they are recognized as such is the best indication that solutions will be found. The problem of the proper distribution of the available catch is being considered, the most advanced resources of the world's most technologically advanced nation are being committed to the increased propagation of the salmon run, and everywhere the vigilant eyes of the sportsmen and ecologists are on the politicians to make sure that this valuable asset of the Columbia is not lightly frittered away.

Salmon forever? I think so. As my old Finn said, "Fish and dis river, dey go togedder." No one better qualified could have said it or said it more eloquently.

River of the Future

THE GEOLOGICAL AGE OF THE Columbia, we are told, is approximately seventy-five million years, in which time it has seen some monumental changes. Yet very possibly no century has had as great an impact on the life of this stream as the last, when the hand of man was first laid on the River and changed it from a wild, untamed giant to a docile series of slackwater pools impounded by artificial mountains of steel and concrete. In one century the number of people living on the banks of the Columbia has gone from a few thousand to well over a million, and industries that did not even exist anywhere in the world now dot its banks in profusion. The natural question is, what does the future hold in store for the Columbia?

Of course, no one knows with absolute certainty what the future holds, but some remarkably astute guesses based on presently available information are possible. That the changes will be many and far reaching is a certainty, and yet the basic quality of the River, its beauty, will most probably remain. So many people appreciate the Columbia's beauty that any change that would greatly diminish it would be fiercely

By midsummer, the banks of the Middle River, as in this scene near Lyle, Washington, turn a tawny gold. This section of the River is often compared to the Nile's Nubian reaches.

resisted. Beauty of this sort is a precious commodity in a world becoming increasingly tawdry as the trappings of civilization take their inevitable toll.

What about technological changes? Again, they will be many, the most important of which will probably be cheap and inexhaustible solar power which will make the hydrological generation of electricity economically unfeasible. So, will the great dams of the Columbia become monuments to a primitive form of energy generation? Hardly that. Most of the dams on the Columbia are multipurpose dams, and energy generation is only one of their many functions. As long as rain falls, snow melts in the mountains, and man needs water, the dams on the Columbia will serve useful purposes in mitigating floods, furnishing irrigation water, and controlling a river that in its natural state was often a social and ecological disaster. The life span of a concrete dam is practically infinite, and barring some unforeseen technological development that would make flood control and irrigation superflous, the dams will probably still be here centuries from now, still performing useful functions and serving as monuments to the hard work and foresight of generations long since turned to dust.

The methods of generating electrical energy will undoubtedly change, and water in the twenty-sixth century may very well be much too precious a commodity to run through a primitive or even contemporary turbine. For all that matter, electrical energy itself may be supplanted by other, more advanced forms of energy radiation. An obvious and welcome change will be more efficient forms of transporting energy, either through fiber optics embedded in the ground or through orbiting satellites that will make obsolete the steel towers and transmission lines that, though useful or even essential, constitute a visual blight on so many otherwise superb Northwest landscapes. Farming methods, feeling the forward thrust of an ever-advancing technological revolution, will undoubtedly be drastically changed, but water is the very basis of life as we know it and so will be as essential ten centuries from now as it is today, even if only for drinking. And the River will be there to supply it.

Of one thing we can be reasonably sure. The Columbia will probably be cleaner a century from now than it is today. A heightened awareness of the value clean water has for our health and environment will undoubtedly spur efforts to remove the last bit of artificial or even natural pollution from the Columbia. That it can be done is well illustrated by the example of the Willamette, a few years ago a running sewer, which today runs so clean and free of pollution that it teems with healthy trout; and the salmon run that had been exterminated by the massive doses of effluent issuing from the towns and industries along its banks has been successfully reestablished. The day is hopefully not so far off when a water skier spilling into the River will laughingly drink down the mouthful of water he has ingested without the slightest fear of diarrhea.

The River's potential for recreation will most likely to be developed far beyond its present state. A clean river suitable for all sorts of water sports will undoubtedly be subjected to very heavy usage by a population increasingly freed from the humdrum necessity of working many hours to make a living. Those extra leisure hours will be spent somewhere: why not on the banks of a beautiful, crystal clear river running through the sun belt? Water sports have been with us ever since the first cave man accidentally fell into a stream on a hot day and found out it not only was not lethal, but actually fun. There is no reason to believe these sports will be any less popular in the future than they are right now, and as the quality of the River increases, so will its recreational uses.

One usage of the River that may actually decrease in the future is in the field of transportation—at least in its present form. Anything that floats displaces water, which is very heavy. Pushing anything through water takes a lot of energy and becomes increasingly difficult at high speeds. Maybe some day large cargo craft may hover over the river as a flat, convenient highway to the sea, but the present slow though efficient towboats will most likely within a century join the paddlewheel steamers as one more chapter in the colorful history of transportation on the Great River. Of course there undoubtedly will be technological improvements in water transportation, and the River may very well be, in centuries to come, a still convenient and busy highway to the sea, but chances are the vessels' form will be so different from the towboats and barges of today as to be almost completely unrecognizable.

The atomic complex at Hanford, already riding a wave of expansion, will certainly grow into one of the greatest research and development centers of the world, especially with the development of the fusion rather than the present fission system of generating atomically powered energy. Hanford simply has so much momentum in the burgeoning field of atomic research that its position is almost certainly assured. The development of the future will concentrate on utilizing the solar radiation that reaches this planet in a way that will not add to the total thermal content of the atmosphere, as present thermal methods do. The danger of adding heat units to the atmosphere, where they conceivably could alter the delicate balance that makes this planet viable, is probably understood no place on Earth better than at Hanford; and while the scientists there are willing to accept the fission and fusion processes as interim sources of power, they know that the only ultimately safe method of power generation in the quantities needed in say, the twenty-sixth century, is the utilization of the vast energy daily pouring onto our planet from the sun.

THE EMPHASIS FOR the next century or so will most probably be on research and the full development of the potential inherent in the atom, but not necessarily for solely atomic energy, and hopefully not for nuclear warfare. By the next century, man should have realized that atomic warfare using the sophisticated weapons available today is tantamount to planetary suicide and have eschewed it as a method of settling national differences. Allowed to progress along the paths of peace, atomic research can unlock untold opportunities in the world of tomorrow . . . and Hanford holds the key. Atomic energy is already acknowledged to be a temporary step toward the ultimate energy, solar power, albeit a very necessary and timely one. Still, the people of the twenty-first century should still be enjoying the desert sun at Richland, basking around their swimming pools and tennis courts and enjoying the good life on the banks of the Columbia, for the River, unlike the vagaries of technology, will always be there, as long as rain falls, snow melts, and water runs downhill.

One aspect of the River will definitely change: there are already straws in the wind. As little as twenty years ago, long stretches of the River were completely devoid of human habitation. Now, here and there, houses are being built on the River which exploit the beauty of a particularly beautiful vista or a singularly attractive beach. Once the Columbia, tamed behind its concrete barriers, ceased to be a flood hazard, its banks became exceptionally attractive building sites, and handsome homes are being built in what was, only a few years ago, a completely unpopulated stretch of river. The trend will undoubtedly escalate, for the Columbia offers vistas of incomparable beauty, and in a society where natural beauty is becoming an increasingly rare commodity, such sites will necessarily command a premium price and be quickly snapped up. The presence of an increasingly frenetic social pace will demand some kind of anodyne, and here on the banks of a beautiful river with the wild wind singing its eternal song, one can find the peace that is so elusive in urban areas.

One place where building should certainly be restricted is the Columbia Gorge. No house, no matter how beautiful, could possibly add to the beauty of this area. It is best left in a natural state so that generations yet unborn may some day be thrilled by the same natural wonders that enthralled Lewis and Clark. Tastefully done parks that utilize the natural beauty of the Gorge have been proven to be no deterrent to the full enjoyment of the wonders so lavishly displayed there, and as population pressures increase, more of them will be necessary. The precedent for these has already been set, and hopefully the designers of the future will follow in the footsteps of those who, in the present day, have successfully blended natural beauty with heavy usage by people.

What about industries along the Columbia? Almost certainly, there will be more of them, because as the waters of the Columbia become less polluted, industries using large quantities of clean water will be attracted to the area. These industries in themselves will be part of the reason for the biggest change that will overtake the River of the future, for in centuries to come, almost certainly there will be cities on the Columbia that are not even hamlets today. As demographic changes accrue, the Northwest, still a comparatively empty part of the United States, will become much more densely populated, and inevitably some of that population will live along the Columbia. This larger population will make different demands on the River than are made today, and the River of the future will necessarily be tuned to those demands.

Circle irrigation has made possible the remarkable transformation of desert to verdant farmland, can be seen at this farm near Boardman, Oregon.

The Middle and Lower Columbia teem with
sailboats. This one is near Hood River.

There will be a greater use of the River for recreation and for municipal water supplies, with all the ecological provisions that presupposes. Pollution control will have to be applied on a massive scale, but the result can only be a cleaner, better, more viable river.

The change that will be evident in all phases of human endeavor along the River will nowhere be more marked than in the second oldest activity of man – agriculture. Even in the twenty-sixth century, man will still have to eat and there still will be farmers furnishing food for the myriad people laboring in the industrial complexes along the River. The farms of the future will be vastly more efficient and mechanized than those of the present, and will probably make extensive use of hydroponics – a step already taken today, when the coarse black sands of the Columbia Basin often are nothing more than a physical support system for vegetables drawing all their nutrients from chemicals sprayed on them from a center pivot irrigation system. The basic ingredients will still be water, sunlight, and the appropriate nutrients for a wide variety of food crops which will be grown in compact, highly efficient blocks utilizing the abundant sunlight of the desert and water pumped from the River. Efficient greenhouses will make a twelve-month growing season feasible, effectively divorcing the growing period from the usual restrictions of the calendar year. The only things that are absolutely essential for successful growing are sunlight, water, and the proper growing environment, and these the lands adjacent to the River can provide in abundance.

In 2500 A.D., citizens will hopefully still be fishing for steelhead and salmon in a rejuvenated River. The food resources of the Columbia are simply too great to be mindlessly destroyed, and a population constantly more mindful of ecological considerations simply will insist on doing whatever is necessary to preserve the fish runs of the Columbia. The hatchery program will be perfected and intensified, most likely with a generation of superfish such as has already been developed at the University of Washington, where salmon are now bred that return from the sea not in the usual four years but in three, even two years, and they are whoppers! There is no reason why the advances in genetics that have been so successful in breeding super plants, super trees, and greatly improved strains of cattle cannot also be applied to

fish life; the result could be a volume of fish similar to what the River bred back in the days when its waters could be drunk from source to mouth. That day can return, although probably not during the lifetime of anyone living in this century. Still, steps have been taken in the right direction and will inevitably continue. Whole sections of the River may be gigantic fish farms where fish are commercially raised, just as cattle are today. The idea is by no means far-fetched: it is already being done in some southern parts of the United States and has been done in Thailand and China for centuries.

There still will be fishermen on the Columbia in centuries to come, although they probably won't have to work nearly as hard to harvest their catch as today's fishermen do. Chances are that through the application of future technologies, there will be enough fish to satisfy the commercial fishermen, the Indians, and the sportsmen alike, so that in 2500 A.D. someone can brag about the big one that broke his pole after having torn through a fisherman's net. The gradual heating of the river through the action of sunlight on water slowed down into slack-water pools – and it is happening – will make feasible the introduction of new, warmer-water species, some of which are already well established on the Snake, and will provide additional sport for light-tackle fishermen.

The problems brought on by the ecological changes caused by the dams on the Columbia were caused by technology, and technology will have to supply the necessary remedies or accommodation. First, a one-degree change in the overall temperature of the River would, on a long-term basis, create some changes in the ecological balance of the River, but nothing really drastic. Such fluctuations have happened many times in the history of the River, and it has always survived. Second, opponents of nuclear energy cite with horror the fact that the Hanford Works contribute about one pound of uranium per day to the Columbia. The River is being "poisoned." What is ignored or unknown to them is that the River has, for untold eons, transported over five hundred pounds of natural uranium every day with absolutely no deleterious effect. Third, agricultural wastes pouring into the River may trigger a sudden growth of algae, which because it is obnoxious and conspicuous, immediately becomes a cause of alarm. Algae has been growing in the Columbia in more or less profusion for centuries, and the

River has survived. What probably will happen is that the River will be subjected to much more stringent observation and control in centuries to come, as its ecological and aesthetic value is more and more appreciated. And that control is not necessarily bad, as long as it is done within limits and with the River's well-being in mind. An uncontrolled River, like an uncontrolled fire, can be a social disaster.

Yes, there will be changes in the Columbia River, but basically it will still be what it is today: a living, pulsating entity stretching from the mountains of Canada to the glistening Pacific and bestowing everywhere the largess of a beauty that is timeless. The moon will still shine on its silvery waters through a crenellated bank of stark basalt cliffs, the waterfalls of the Gorge will still thunder into the River from cliffs hundreds of feet high, and the sandy islands of the Columbia will still play host to hundreds of happy picnickers. Even in 2500 A.D. the desert sun will blaze down pitilessly from a brazen sky over the desert stretches of the River, and the wild winter winds will howl banshee-like through the Gorge. And in the Delta, the mists will rise from the waters as they have from time immemorial.

And should those mists form themselves into the ghostly shapes of Lewis and Clark, the voyageurs, and the myriad men and women whose lives have been touched by this, their beloved Columbia River, they would look upon a River ever changing, yet basically the same, ever old, yet ever new, and always, timelessly, beautiful.

And they would be glad.

Index

ACKNOWLEDGMENTS

UNDERTAKING A PROJECT as comprehensive as the story of a mighty river is not a simple task and was not accomplished without considerable help from the people who made up the gist of this story. In looking over my notes, I find the names of over 1,200 people, each of whom is worthy of mention, who have in some way assisted me in the making of this book.

To each one of you, I give my sincere, heartfelt thanks. While good manners would dictate that individual thanks should be given to all, the mind recoils in horror at the magnitude of this task. Also, my editor has assigned me one page, no more, for what could become a tome of some considerable length.

To somewhat solve this problem and obviate the opening of what could become a barrel of snakes, I will rely on generalities and beg the indulgence of those people who so generously gave me of their time and effort, and so helped to make this work possible.

My thanks go to those administrators of the River, the Corps of Engineers, the Bureau of Reclamation, various PUDs, British Columbia Hydro, and all their employees, who to a man and woman gave me all the help for which a person could ask. Whether it was getting permission to visit some part of the project usually off limits to nonemployees, or giving my kayak a lift around some dam that was blocking my progress downstream, these people were invariably helpful and cooperative.

My special thanks also go to the Bonneville Power Administration without whose help this project would have been much more difficult and not nearly as comprehensive. An ancillary benefit from my association with the BPA has been the formation of several friendships that have considerably enriched my life.

Not all my benefactors were highly placed. I remember boats being placed at my disposal, lock-tenders who were sympathetic and helpful, local information freely given, and offers of help with almost any problem I faced in my various trips up and down the River. The fact that some of that information was not too accurate and nearly cost a couple of lives is not too important: the information was given with the intention of helping us, and that is what I most remember.

I think it is only right that I should burnish the escutcheon of an organization whose reputation certainly need no further embellishment, but richly deserves it: The Royal Canadian Mounted Police. Whether they were bending the rules a bit to allow me to carry a heavy handgun in grizzly country—something somewhat frowned upon by Canadian law—or checking on my welfare by helicopter after I had been out of touch with civilization for a few days, I have found these men to be every bit as good as their legend.

When I was doing research on the Columbia, I was amazed at the paucity of printed matter on the whole stream. Technical journals, of course, were in profusion, and some parts of the River, notably the Columbia Gorge had been heavily covered, but hundreds of miles of the River were relatively unknown and unheralded. There were, however, some good books, done many years ago before the River was bound in chains of steel and concrete, which correctly caught the mystique of this beautiful stream, and so became part of the background knowledge that is so necessary in a project of this sort. My thanks and admiration go to authors long dead who would understand completely how enchanted I became with this beautiful river.

I must also acknowledge the help of various historical associations and libraries, especially the British Museum, for bending their usually stringent regulations, so that I was able to peruse books and records which, in some instances, had not been opened for over one hundred years.

Last, but certainly not least, I must acknowledge the contributions of those intrepid explorers, voyageurs, fur traders, and missionaries whose journals, both in French and English have done so much to instill in me the knowledge that I am neither the first to fall under the spell of the Columbia, nor will I be the last. I will be very proud to have my book placed next to theirs under the heading "Columbia River."